C000212415

52 Greek Islands

A sentimental journey

THIRD EDITION - 2019

52 Greek Islands

A sentimental journey

Copyright: Strange days books & Gregory Papadoyiannis
www.strangedaysbooks.gr
www.paraxenesmeres.gr

Publishing advisor: Andriana Minou

ext and photos of the book: Gregory Papadoyiannis
https://gregorypapadoyiannis.wordpress.com/

Editor: Christina Markanastasakis
Translators: Georgia Alexiou
            Danae Roussou

First edition: summer 2013
Second edition: spring 2016
Third edition: spring 2019
Cover photo: Schinoussa
Back cover: Tilos

Strange days books,
ISBN-13: 9781092487603
(CreateSpace-Assigned)

52 Greek Islands

Contents

PREFACE FOR THE NEW EDITION

Six years after the first *52 islands* edition many things have changed in Greece but relatively very few of them have to do with the islands, with the exception that some of them especially at the north part of the Aegean Sea like Lesvos, Chios, Leros and a few others served as the temporary resort for refugees from the Syrian war. But as almost nothing is temporary in this country many of them are still there and unfortunately suffering from a lot of problems especially in the winter.

Apart from this, the idea for this new edition is to have a "lighter" version of it, that is less sentimental and more - let's say- to the point. And the point is the islands. So there are some changes but not at the essence of the book, which is always to have a different guide from the usual, a guide that tells you everything about the islands, both the beautiful and the ugly side of them - when there is one. To put it better I prefer the words that Lane Ashfeldt –an excellent author and a woman who knows Greece very well- wrote about this book: *At last: a no-spoilers guidebook. This could be a thing.*

Many more photos, less sentiment and two more islands - little ones- in this edition. So it is not actually 52 of them but neither am I 52 years old anymore. No need to change the title. Let's keep it between us!

52 Islands

INTRODUCTION

This is a "sentimental" guide for travellers, through 52 of the Greek islands. The term "sentimental guide" implies something more than a commonplace guide and I assure you that my book is not written in the style of a classic guidebook. There is already a plethora of classic guidebooks; the internet is rife with a lot of useful – yet even more useless – information. This book has simply been written out of an outrageous love for the islands, to describe of what it feels like to actually "live the island" – even for a week – and to find out what it's like, from how it looks to how it can be characterized in terms of its deeper essence. I liken this process to getting to know a friend, or perhaps even falling in love.

Travelling around means you need resources like time and money. But isn't this also the way when it comes to creating friendships? It takes time to get to know someone, and furthermore, you need to be in the mood for this, to love him/her and enjoy his/her company. This is what happened in my relationship with the islands. Throughout all these years of my travels, most of the islands have changed, but then show me a friend of yours who hasn't changed with the passage of time. Of course, nothing compares to the feeling of getting to know a new island, when you first see the lights in the middle of the night as the ship approaches the port. Then there's the wonderful feeling of seeing an island, just like with your dearest old friends. That's because every island is a unique creature, and all the islands are somehow just one island – this is what I've felt, even from the beginning. The same applies to humans.

What you will find here

For every island, you will find information about its history and its connection with the other islands which belong to the same group.

You will also find basic information about how to get around and spots that I think you should not miss, in order to get a complete picture and enjoy your stay on the island. Keep in mind that this is a guide for travellers and not for ordinary tourists. As such, what I believe is most significant is to give you information based on my own experience, about the style, character, profile and personality of each island.

Along with the commentary on the islands, this book contains some basic yet essential tips for travellers to Greece – and particularly for those travelling to the islands. Moreover, there is a small section with some tips – one might say an emotional survival guide – for all those who need to know what to do during their first day on an island.

What you will not find

You won't find recommendations about the best restaurant, the best night club or the best hotel on each island. This information can be accessed using many other resources. This is not a book containing typical advice for tourists and not just another classic travel guide for the Greek islands; there are already plenty of excellent ones to choose from. This is something unique that cannot be found anywhere else; it is a sentimental journey through the Greek islands and I want to share it with you.

Introduction to the Greek Landscape:
GREECE FOR BEGINNERS

A very brief history of modern Greece

Greece has never become what we would call a completely independent country. Since the days of the struggle for independence (1821-1829) hitherto, Greece has lived only a few bright oases of independence but has always been subject to the supervision (to say the least) of nations considered to be world powers, which in any case imposed the conditions under which they guaranteed Greece's independence. This significant page of modern Greek history – the struggle for independence – has ended with foreign stamps and signatures.

The first governor of the modern Greek state and Greece's independence – Ioannis Kapodistrias – tried to create an independent path for this country and was murdered. The fact that he was murdered by Greeks is ultimately of little significance. His murder was extremely convenient for some of the local population and even more for the foreign powers that eschewed the concept that Greece could operate as an independent state.

Following this, Kings were instated who were not even Greeks, and they ruled with little help from miserable politicians – who unfortunately *were* Greeks. Subsequent historical events consist of the expansion of frontiers, retreats, bankruptcies and catastrophes. The dawn of the 20th century brought victorious wars with neighbouring regions and the Asia Minor catastrophe that completely transformed the population of Greece. The First and the Second World Wars were undoubtedly difficult periods for most people in Europe; for Greece the Second World War included the arduous German occupation, followed by a disastrous civil war. Cyprus's struggle for independence followed – in which Greece had some involvement – and then there was the military dictatorship. This was followed by the "comeback" of democracy. However, from 2010 onwards, Greece has been closely monitored by the

International Monetary Fund as a country which is already bankrupt, more or less.

Greece in the years of the crisis
Here we are now, in a very painful period of recession which has gone on for six consecutive years, with millions unemployed (one and a half million officially, although many more in fact – the highest percentage in Europe), thousands homeless and three hundred thousand businesses in ruin within just a few years. Harsh economic measures have been imposed, weighing down the segment of the population that is least responsible for the incredibly wasteful spending in the public sector, which had been going on for years but was especially excessive right before the time that Greece, for all intents and purposes, went bankrupt.

This is Greece: a proud and humiliated country; a country with great people and wretched people; a country full of contradictions. The bad news is that it's not a happy time for Greeks and this won't be changing anytime soon. The good news is that Greece is still a beautiful country, the islands are still marvellous, summer is still magical and, as we said before, the traveller can still enjoy the lovely ambience of life on the islands. Now, what does all of this have to do with you, dear traveller? That's something I will explain to you in the very next section.

The Illegal state
Greece is a country of outlaws. In case that doesn't reassure you, I can tell you that most are just occasional "illegals" that have to be that way mainly because the great ring leader is the Greek state itself – a governing body that compels you to behave illegally in order to survive. A classic example of this is the illegal buildings that are found everywhere. Even government buildings have been built illegally since no one bothers to enforce building regulations. Real power in Greece belongs to no more than a few dozen wealthy families who have arbitrarily built villas

wherever they please because no one dares to check. There are thousands of other arbitrary buildings – from sheds to entire housing settlements – built illegally because there is simply no other way to get things done. In order to obey the laws of this country – a country that doesn't even have a land registry – a citizen must bravely confront nonsensical bureaucracy and arbitrary decisions made by employees of the state. For example, urban planners will request a small "gift" for their services, regardless of whether what you're asking for is legal or illegal. Innocent citizens are then faced with a dilemma: do the right thing and accept that your dream house will remain a dream, or pander to the illicit requests of state employees who hold your fate in their hands. It's not difficult to guess what most people decide to do, and the story does not end here. The buildings, which are then randomly built, will be at risk for all kinds of potential fines for the violation of building regulations. At some point – usually before a critical election – the government will remember what it has to accomplish. And what is this? To secure as many votes as possible. In order to get more votes, they will pass laws to legitimize these illegally built buildings and perhaps impose a few small fines where necessary. So the previously illegal acts are then made legal by the government itself. However, in the meantime, people with years of experience and frustration in these matters will give birth to thousands of other citizens who will eventually become illegals too; the day will come where their illegal acts will be legitimized. And so the cycle continues. This explains why there are so many villas built in areas that were previously forest land – land suspiciously ravaged during forest fires and conveniently left bereft of trees. There are resorts that have been illegally built on the seaside and factories (when there were still factories in Greece) that have been established in urban areas without a hitch. All of these actions have implications for the environment, including dwindling forests and the violation of what should be protected areas. Of course, everyone in the country has to put up with the ugliness of these buildings, which have been erected adjacent to streams, rivers, lakes and beaches. This is how things are and the only saving grace is that this country has plenty of beauty; they haven't managed to wipe all of it out yet. However, this will be discussed below. Over the last thirty years, 4,000 new laws have been voted on and 110,000 ministerial decrees have been published. The result is a maze of laws that often negate each other and remain at the discretion of each state employee to apply as he or she chooses.

Perhaps the most intelligent quotation about this situation has been written by poet George Souris (from the island Syros, see below) who said, one hundred and thirty years ago, that: *"Greece does not need other laws. / It has too many. / It just needs a law that requires them to apply the ones that already exist."*

The 'We' utopia

Nobody can say for sure who started it, and it's not very important anyway. Were the citizens of the country the ones who sought the easy way out, or did the government provide an easy solution to its "favourite children"? The establishment of the independent Greek state gave rise to one very important distinction from the very beginning, which is that there are two kinds of people: "our" people and the others. "Our" people are those who willingly pay homage to the flag of a political party and even more simply, make themselves available to be of service to a corrupt politician, knowing full well that the reward will come soon afterwards. That's how it is. The "our children" are appointed to the state as employees, get favours whenever they have a "problem" with the government or other citizens, acquire fortunes that are never audited, even commit quite simple illegal acts, like running a red light, confident with the knowledge that even if it doesn't go unnoticed, they will be let off scot-free, because a phone call will be made to declare that they are one of "our" people in the municipal office, the police, the tax bureau and so on. Does this seem backward to you? Well it's just the truth.

12

Nobody can really say if it was corrupt politicians who kicked off this way of doing things, or whether the citizens were seeking to be corrupted. The issue is that after centuries of legalized corruption nobody trusts anybody. Both classes of citizens, both those who "wheel and deal" with politicians and those who refuse to engage in such activities, know one thing very well: whatever they do, they do for themselves and their close relatives. These are the limits of "we" in Greece. All the others are potential enemies until proven otherwise. And the biggest enemy of them all is the government. So the "we" is absent in relation to collective responsibility, genuine social movements and team efforts geared toward the greater good. Greece is comprised of many small islets of selfishness. Of course there are also many islets of solidarity, but these are doomed to make progress on a very small scale. So it's not at all unusual to see someone opening the window of his car and emptying the ashtray of cigarette butts onto the road, or pouring out his unfinished coffee onto the sidewalk, or throwing his emptied soda can into the sea. All you to need to know – and this is by no means a justification – is that this man has grown up believing that the mess he leaves on the road, in the sea and in everything around him will have to be cleaned up by someone else

This man has learned to live with the motto "every man for himself and the government against all." It's no wonder that with indifference he mixes up what "we" means in relation to the problems of society in general, which could be faced collectively. He hasn't learned to respect anything beyond himself because he's a man that no one has shown respect to. Thus, every form of social expression confirms the attitude: "I can throw my garbage anywhere and someone else will simply have to clean it up."

Too much beauty to handle

A very good example of how the Greek government does things relates to "green cleaning." After putting it off as long as possible, Greece was forced to get into gear on the issue of cleaning up the environment in the 1990's and only did so because the European Commission threatened to impose very severe financial penalties. Even then, the government and local authorities contrived a system designed to deal with the problem and meet the EC's minimum requirements. Once these were fulfilled, the system and all efforts were abandoned (this is not at all an uncommon approach to many problems). Subsequently, the authorities simply became indifferent to the problem until the day that a "bad" foreigner found out what was going on and filed a case against Greece, which reawakened the threat of penalties and fines. Greece has been referred to the European Court of Justice – and found to be in violation of European law – on numerous occasions on many similar issues.

It is estimated that 80% of cities with more than 15,000 residents (and a mere 20% of cities with 2,000 to 15,000 residents) are currently receiving service from wastewater treatment plants. Even if the national government makes decisions about things, local authorities do not take into account the operational and maintenance costs of executing these decisions. The result is that these services start to wane or even come to a complete halt. As such, the phenomenon reappears in some towns and villages, that although there seems to be a range of wastewater treatment facilities, the sewage ends up in the rivers, lakes and sea once again. This is an extremely unpleasant image and certainly does not assist you in enjoying your dream holiday in Greece. However, it sometimes happens.

Almost exactly the same approach has been taken by the national government in relation to the Greek Natura 2000 areas, which no doubt have been badly affected by the financial crisis. It has become nearly impossible for the government to provide funding to these areas and maintain them, and it has been officially stated that: "it is very unlikely that the national government will be able to provide funds for this purpose at this time." The fact that this specific goal – the protection and enhancement of the environment – could give rise to huge profits (assuming that you're trying to think as they do) is not an issue for them. In fact, I believe that those who govern Greece have something worse than indifference to the environment: they unconsciously hate things which relate to beauty, because authentic beauty is beyond their comprehension – it is simply over their heads. Fortunately, there is still plenty of natural beauty here. There are four hundred and nineteen Natura 2000 sites in Greece occupying approximately forty-three thousand square kilometers, seven thousand of which are marine areas. But how long can "development" be sustained – that is, exploitation without consequences? A few months ago, a mayor on one of the Ionian Islands was celebrating after selling a piece of land classified as a Natura 2000 area to foreign investors. According to the statement he made to the press, the mayor was excited because: "now there will be development and they will build a palace there." Was he ignoring the fact that it is not permitted to build anything in these areas, except, perhaps, a wooden shack? Probably not. That's the worst part about it.

BASIC TIPS FOR TRAVEL

Booking, booking, booking

Yes, I know you have this in mind. I just want to be sure that you have taken steps to make an advance booking for a hotel room or a room in a guesthouse or wherever you intend to stay. No doubt you have already booked your flight to Greece. What I would mainly like to talk about are the ferry tickets that you will need to travel from Athens (Pireaus) to the island you want to go to, or any tickets you might need to transfer to other islands. If you can book these tickets in advance, definitely do it. Be aware that booking a ticket is even more difficult on the small ferries that are often used between islands and sometimes advance reservations can't be made. So if you are unable to book your ticket to a neighbouring island in advance, be sure to buy it as soon as you've set foot on your destination. This is particularly important if you come to the Greek islands during the hot season. But what does hot really mean on a Greek island?

The hot season

You know, of course, what the expression "hot season" means. This is the period between mid-July and mid-August. However, you will not understand the meaning of "popular island in Greece" until you've actually stayed there and lived it for a while. For those who haven't experienced this yet, I have this to say: "hot season" on the Greek islands means, above all, too many people. In other words, a few million tourists scattered mainly on Crete, Rhodes, Corfu, Paros, Mykonos and Santorini and a lot of overcrowding issues. This is also the case on other islands that share these problems, on a smaller scale of course. I have already emphasized the importance of booking tickets sooner rather than later. Use this as a general guideline. Be sure to reserve your seat at the "tourist party." Not only on ferries and at hotels, but also in tavernas, cafes, clubs, discos, buses, cars rental shops and so on. They will be bustling with people and not only that. Even if you reserve your seat, be aware that the space will be cramped on excursions, guided tours, beaches, and even at secluded (well, until the hot season!) beaches frequented by nudists. It's this overcrowding which seriously comprises the quality of services on offer. There are no statistics on this, but think of it this way: if a taverna is full of people (if you are among the lucky ones who have a table) the service will be incredibly slow and will not be what it could have been. The food will not be what it could have been. Even the waiter's smile will not be as broad as it could have been – in fact, it might be non-existent. Try to see it from their point of view: most of these people live off of tourism. They endure endless months of a desolate winter, followed by some relatively pleasant months of tourism, followed by the panic of the hot season. Is it even possible for someone to prepare for this? Not really. They must get out of their usual rhythm in order to accommodate as many people as possible, so they can make up the balance for the money they don't earn during the months when there isn't tourism. They can't do otherwise, which immediately takes us to the next topic.

I'm not what I say
This is a key aspect of the Greek temperament: pretending to be something other than what you actually are. In the tourism sector, things like greed, a lack of rules or the failure to apply existing rules have created a series of issues in which the truth is often stretched or covered up, so that the quickest and easiest profit can be made.
To be fair, things have changed for the better over the last two decades. But there are still numerous greedy characters around and a lot of ways to trick unsuspecting tourists – and not just foreigners. A good example of progress that has been made is that finally there are signs posted at the main gateways of the capital (ports, train stations, airports) that clearly indicate taxi prices. Quite a few tall tales have been told about shrewd taxi drivers, who in the past would ask for exorbitant amounts from innocent tourists. This behaviour has been more or less eradicated,

but make sure to check these signs wherever they exist just to be on the safe side, and make sure to drop by the offices of EOT (the Greek Tourism Organization) when you arrive on an island (wherever there is one) and as a simple rule, I would advise you to always ask the taxi driver what the fare will be for your journey at the very start.

Not always fresh
A tourist's desire to taste the local specialties is always respected; it could not be otherwise. Obviously, when you're in a country like Greece and especially on an island, you'd like to try, for example, some fresh fish. Island plus sea plus fishing should equal fresh fish on your plate. This should be the equation but it's not always the rule, and this could especially be the case if you come from a country where you haven't developed the ability to discern the taste of fresh fish. So bear in mind the previous chapter ("I'm not what I say") and consider that managing to get fresh fish on your plate may not be the easiest thing to do. This may be especially true in places where there are a lot of tourists and only a few fishermen. In truth, it's only when you know the taste of really fresh fish that you can determine whether fish served to you at a taverna isn't fresh, even though that's what you've paid for. Chances are that you are even eating frozen fish. Bear in mind therefore, that "small is beautiful" and in order to get authentic tastes of local food you should pick small tavernas that bring in the "catch of the day." Also you should know that the small fish (sardines, anchovies, etc.) can't be frozen. If they are on the menu, they're fresh. Another good rule to follow is that you can always trust a taverna owner who has said, at one point or another, that "today there is no fresh fish." This could happen, for example, when the sea is rough and the fishermen can't go out. When there's been stormy weather for a few days, the rule is: never eat fish. If you ask for fresh fish on a day with stormy weather, an authentic taverna owner might even get angry at you for your ignorance.
The same applies to meat: remember that dishes made with minced meat are less likely to be made of fresh meat.

Also, it may be obvious, but it is good to remember that there are specific times of the year when fruits and vegetables ripen, and not necessarily when you are visiting an island. That's why they're called seasonal fruits and vegetables. For example: the season for tomatoes is summertime and early autumn (when, as the old saying goes, the tomato has gathered all the sun) rather than in winter. Winter tomatoes ripen in greenhouses, and for this reason they are very different. You should know that "wild greens" brought to you in summer probably aren't fresh, in the same way that vine leaves are picked in summer, and so the dish "stuffed vine leaves" is fresh in summer but probably made of frozen vine leaves in winter and spring.

And now the bill…
Last year a new law was adopted in Greece (in an effort to "fight fraud" as they say) that requires shop owners to provide customers with receipts. In Greece, providing a receipt is not as obvious as you may think and this is due to a number of factors. The law states that if a receipt is not given, a customer is not obligated to give payment. This is also indicated at cash machines. However, I beg you: do not even consider doing this! In any case, you are no doubt interested in getting good value for money. So assuming that they bring you the bill (probably with a receipt), you must carefully read it (I assume that at the very least, there will be an English translation of the menu). There is no shame in ensuring that you pay them just for what you bought. Getting charged extra is the exception and not the rule. In any event, things have improved and the bills normally correspond with the food consumed. But again, all rules have their exceptions. And now bear in mind three very simple tips; try to remember them. It is good to avoid the hot season if you really want to get to know a Greek island. First, it is also advisable, if you can, to avoid the most popular islands during all three summer months and aim to book your holiday there during late spring or early autumn. These are the best months for travellers visiting Greece. Secondly, try

to observe which shops and tavernas the local residents go to and choose those ones as the quality will be pretty much guaranteed – unless what you are looking for can't be found at the small, well-kept taverna or coffee bar preferred by locals. Generally, it's a good idea to avoid places that are full of tourists. I know that you're a tourist but you're also a traveller. Thirdly, a bit of advice that might seem somewhat strange to you: do not trust – at least not on the very first day of your trip – the simple, friendly, cordial fellow who may approach you with the best intentions to help you. He might actually have the best intentions. But it is very likely that he just wants to "sell" you something, such as a hotel room, a meal at his restaurant, fresh fish, an inflatable raft or whatever else. The era when Greek islanders who approached you had only motives of hospitality has ended. If you want to hang out with someone, don't pick the person who has drawn near you the minute you've set foot on the island – pick someone else. I have a little more advice below regarding your first day on an island. But now please read the next section in order to familiarize yourself with the terminology of this travel guide.

The Lazy tourist and the Beast
The Lazy Tourist is the opposite of the traveller. We talk a lot about the Lazy Tourist in this book: the "tourist-we-don't-want-to-be." He/she is the individual who just wants to consume tourism without bothering to get to know a country or a place. Indeed, all parts of the Earth are the same to the Lazy Tourist. He/she is the individual on which the tourism industry is based and for the traveller serves as an example in order to know what NOT to do.

Who is the "Beast"
This expression is used quite frequently in this guide. But who or what is this monster? It is the heedless "development" of tourism that slowly devours anything authentic on the islands. The economic crisis has offered at least one good thing to Greece and its islands: it has knocked the wind out of the Beast. It hasn't disappeared of

course. The wounds that have been left almost everywhere by the Beast include the joy of the Lazy Tourist which is also the traveller's nightmare. Once again, this book has been written for the traveller. There is frequent reference to places where the Beast has done its damage, so that the traveller can be informed and in a position to decide when it's not even worth setting foot on such places.

But what's the point of talking about all this?

To answer this, dear reader, I must tell you that if you believe that the above information is not relevant to your holiday and if you think that you don't need to know anything about the country you're going to be visiting, then sorry but this book is not for you. I hope you just glance at these words flicking through the book in a bookstore. But don't buy it. And of course you don't need to know anything about the Beast. Even if you came face to face with it, you wouldn't recognize it.

And the Ship Sails ...

We start our journey on the Greek islands. We will ride on an imaginary ship and follow some real routes: the regular routes of the ferries that take you to the islands. First we will sail to the Cyclades, including the small Cyclades islands. Then we will go to the Dodecanese and following this we will journey up to the eastern Aegean, then even further north to the islands in Macedonia and Thrace prefectures. After that we will go down to the Sporades Islands, and then to the islands of the Saronic Gulf. You will need to pass through Athens, but Athens is not an island and does not concern us here. In fact, it would be ideal if you could just make a short stop to see the Acropolis, stay long enough for a quick coffee and stroll around in Plaka or Thissio. That would be enough.

We will only use Athens (Piraeus, actually) as a starting point and will "disembark" at the islands. After we visit the Saronic Gulf islands, there is the huge "island" – the Peloponnese – then we'll cross the Myrtoo Sea and sail to the Ionian islands. For the finale we'll sail to Crete, the

21

island I live on now. I hope you can make the entire trip. Realistically speaking, it's a journey which could take some years or even a lifetime, so the most likely scenario is to travel only to some of the islands listed here. Even so, it is time to start. Just a moment, though. I want to tell you a few words about your first day on the island.

TIPS FOR THE FIRST DAY ON THE ISLAND

The advice I'm about to give you is based purely on sentiment, but then again, what isn't in this book? Well, my advice is to ignore the alleged difficulties and arrive on the island at nighttime. I assume that you'll go there by ferry – a night ferry, let's say. So if you want to make it a little more difficult, you'll approach the island late at night. Okay, I know it is not the easiest thing to do. There are issues with checking into hotels and rooms late at night, but I still recommend it. We're travellers aren't we?

Next, buy a map of the island. There are usually inexpensive maps (in tourist shops), there are very good maps (look in places where they sell newspapers) and there are tourist maps – the ones highlighting coffee shops and tavernas. Remember that the latter are not the best – the shops have paid those who make the maps for advertising. So, forget the third category and select from the first two.

And now I'll ask you to do something strange. Read the map – the map you bought in multilingual version I suppose – read it carefully or even better, "travel" within that map and then set it aside. You have the book, you have your instincts and that's more than enough. Try to get by without it and open it only when you need help finding your way on the road or for longer distances. But first, find out what interests you most on this island. Would that be small remote beaches that can only be accessed by small boats? Rugged mountains and canyons? Picturesque villages? Ancient ruins? Whatever it is that you want, try to find and enjoy it "without instructions." You won't need them, you just need to feel the very essence of the living creature, as every island is a living creature. Then begin. If you feel somewhat insecure, take the map with you. Start though.

CYCLADES

Kythnos

"Kythnos" is not the first hat (or car) that an ordinary salesperson would bring out for you to see. He would want to show you some flashier models first, because that's how he learnt to do things. In the same way, no travel guide for the Greek islands starts off with Kythnos – no one would even think of beginning with this island. In the best case scenario, it would be mentioned in conjunction with other islands. Also, it's highly unlikely that anyone would ever send you a postcard from Kythnos bearing the message: "We've had a fabulous time, it's out of this world, unbelievable things happen here!" even if in reality he/she had actually had a great time.

In any case, we're not in the business of selling cars here and this is a totally different kind of travel guide. We've got some road ahead of us and we may as well do things right. The itinerary that we're about to follow can actually be done. It might seem too good to be true (and too adventurous for that matter), but depending on circumstances, is definitely possible. With this in mind, I shall kick off our journey, departing from Piraeus and heading toward Kythnos.

Kythnos has the tumultuous fate of that schoolgirl (or schoolboy) that let you have your way with her without having to make very much effort. That's what she was bound to do, simply because she liked you. She would be your first love. Similarly, Kythnos is the first stop in your love affair with the Cyclades, when you take the ferry from Piraeus (or alternatively from the port of Lavrio, from which the island is only two hours away). And we all know what happens next. Even though she is beautiful and unique and wonderful in every way possible, she is destined to be forgotten; buried deep in a box labelled "fleeting loves" (if you can even be bothered to label that box) and placed on a dusty shelf in the back corner of your memory. But Kythnos is worth far more than that. For the sake of this island and for the sake of all your loves that you never gave real affection to, I'm going to spend a lot of time telling you about Kythnos. And I'm not only going to make it the first stop on our route, I'm also going to tell you a little bit more about it relative to other islands. With Kythnos as the impetus, I'm going to explain a few more things now at the beginning, which may come in handy during your entire trip.

Here's another one of its advantages: since it's the first island on the ferry route, this means that there will be no unpredictable – albeit common – delays at the ports, especially if you have taken fast ferries. This is due to the fact that a journey which stops at many ferry ports (given that you've ignored the advice) usually means a trip which is more or less longer from that which was promised to you, and there is nothing romantic about this.

I've been to Kythnos many times. The last time was during the period that my daughter was born. I knew that it was the end of an era – I had finally come round to that choice, which had taken me many years to make. I knew that from then on, I wouldn't have the unbridled freedom to travel to the islands, alone, in love, or in search of love – ultimately in search of love for the islands. I chose Kythnos for my final farewell trip, and just for one day. Why's that? Because – as I told you before – it's the past loves that always remain available. It was my past love that was waiting for me – calm, sweet, meek and indifferent to the fake accessories worn by the rest. Kythnos has its own authenticity – but like everything authentic, it never flaunts it nor provokes you to go looking for it. If you're a real traveller, you'll find it.

There is absolutely nothing pretentious about Kythnos. The Beast has passed – you can see its claw-marks (the bamboo seating and plastic loungers, a disjointed building, a house built right on the sand) – but for reasons you can easily surmise, it didn't stay long. Kythnos managed to bamboozle it and escape with few wounds, by posing as an ordinary island. Yet it isn't.

Do you honestly want to feel the essence of a Cycladic island? Are you even more interested in finding out about life there? Remember what I asked you at the beginning: do you know exactly what you want from the islands? If you do, ignore the myths created by advertising and you will find it, here on Naxos, Serifos, Syros and a whole lot of other islands. You will need to search for it a little bit more deeply; don't go looking for the images shown in ads. Like everything created by advertising, these images lack real essence, they're flimsy and ultimately void. If you want holidays without essence, then simply bypass these islands. There are other islands that are reminiscent of a movie set – just try not to peek behind it.

I was telling you about Kythnos. If you like its "touristy" side, its façade which remains more or less unchanged, then you will no doubt be keen on its other side which is wonderfully authentic (but not traditional, there is a difference), simply genuine and has a completely unique character. I suggest that you take some time to carefully look at the houses lining the street, some of which have been built by Athenians who may or may not originate from Kythnos, and who have made them with all the features that their houses in the capital lack. You'll see beauty, good taste, "meraki" (a word that can roughly be translated as "artistry" but can't really be understood unless you've extensively travelled in "real" Greece), and ultimately another dimension of time, a different perspective about the meaning of life.

I love all the islands. There are some however – as I imagine it happens with children, or with past loves – that you just seem to love a little bit more than the rest. Kythnos is one of those islands. During your trip you will probably understand which ones they are, even without me having to point them out. For Kythnos and for these other ones, love reaches the boundaries of pure adoration and it is so easy to talk about them… The words pour out onto the page effortlessly, one harmoniously following the other, like carefree waves that ceaselessly caress the shore. You can hear its sounds from far away; you can see it without actually being there. That's how I can see, with such incredible ease, the small port of Kythnos, which is nothing special or even very traditional, or worthy of mention, but maybe this is why it's so cherished. I can see the small cafes along the seafront and "Merichas" – the name of the port that welcomes you – the tourist shops on the small hill leading to the road which takes you to the other side of the island, the tavernas with the pergolas, the bakery down the little alley just a few steps from the seafront. I can picture it all and I feel so glad that I got the chance to know it. I proceed up the road toward the interior of the island. The first stop will be for Chora, that's how it always is on islands. It's around 8km away – less than half an hour by bus on the uphill road that travels along endless meadows of dried grass, yellow fields, small patches of green and exquisite mills. On the way, you might see donkeys passing by from time to time. The bus takes me to Chora, with its narrow, paved roads and cobblestone paths that were built four centuries ago. From there, I make my way down to the beach. There are two: the large and the small one, which is ideal for families. Of course, there are plenty more – you just have to look for them. The intrinsic aspect of wind, which could hinder your enjoyment of the beach, is rare on Kythnos. Without doubt, you should visit Kolona – with the islet of Agios Loukas just opposite – and Apokrisi or Apokrousi beach (two words that are written pretty much the same in Greek, but with totally different meanings: response or rejection) with its inviting sand. Kalo Livadi beach will have been already discovered and taken over by the typical, lazy tourists: it is one of the beaches that they prefer. At the same distance from Merichas (8km), you will find the quite picturesque Dryopida beach (you can also visit the huge cave Katafiki, not far away from there) which might be an ideal stop on your way to Kanala village. This area, where the church of its patron saint "Panagia Kanala" stands, is somewhat like the "heart and soul" of the island.

A visit there is also a must. You will experience the ambience of the Cyclades, especially around August 15th, which is the great religious celebration of summer.

For the ancient capital you will have to go to Vriokastro (very close to Merichas port) where you will see ruins, sanctuaries devoted to the goddess Demeter, the foundations of temples and altars, as well as of the town "agora" or market. The village of Loutra (which translated into English means "thermal baths") is at the northeast part of the island. It is a small, appealing village and the choice of the elderly who want to have a holiday. (It should be noted that due to its thermal springs, Kythnos was once known by the name "Thermia"). The ruins of the medieval capital of the island are very close to Loutra village and accessible by footpath, where you can also see the castle of Oria.

But what fascinates me the most at this usually peaceful and quite melancholic place, are the houses which surround it. The majority of them have gardens – some have small yards while others have bigger ones and some of them look like little farms. These are small, simple architectural works of art which you will not find in a lifestyle magazine – they have arisen out of spontaneous human inspiration. It is exactly this which allows you to get the measure of Kythnos and fall in love with it.

Kythnos has the bad luck of being very close to Piraeus (only 3 hours away) and this undoubtedly means – as I've already warned you – that during the hot summer months as well as on weekends throughout the year, it gets inundated with "intruders" from Piraeus. Although many of them do not know why they love Kythnos, most of them leave the island without any special experience with which to impress their friends. Even worse, they swarm the island and prevent you, the traveller, from experiencing the deeper essence of this beloved island. I just hope I've told you enough to convince you that Kythnos is the best proof that happiness may be found in "small" things.

Serifos

Serifos

If Kythnos is the girl who blends into the wallpaper and Sifnos the one that turns heads, Serifos is the nonchalant girl who keeps her distance. Serifos and Sifnos have quite a few things in common, there next to each other on the map. You could say that they are the epitome of the phrase "typical Cycladic islands." They are neither flashy nor overly crowded and while both of them have had a rather benign visit from the Beast, and are reasonably far from Piraeus – a fact that makes them ideal even for weekend getaways.

There is something special about Serifos. It seems somewhat indifferent to your presence and reluctant to welcome visitors. But it is in no way any less impressive once you get to know it. There are people that you don't warm up to at first, but if you bother to get to know them a little… This is how it is with Serifos.

As I was saying earlier, the Beast has not changed many things since the beginning of the 80's, when I first visited the island with a friend and my girlfriend – a combination of people which proved to be a huge mistake. It was then that I realised that there are three ways to visit an island: alone, with many friends, or with the person you are in love with. There is no other way – anything else will just turn out wrong. Back then, three people with completely different tastes did not manage to agree on anything other than the return ticket, as soon as possible. Of course, I visited the island again a few years after that. Things were better for us – both Serifos and me, I mean. As well as with my new girlfriend at that point.

Now let's look at what happened, using Livadi as an example. The first time I went there it was an isolated beach, reminiscent of a desert. We put up our tent in the middle of the beach and that was it. From time to time, some people came to swim. There were kilometres of space for all of us.

The second time, things were different. Livadi (its beach is actually called Avlomonas) was not isolated. Houses had been built nearby, cars frequently roared by just above us;

"caravans" of families came to the beach and spent many, many hours there. The only thing that resembled a desert was the sand. Had it got better? I admit that I preferred the isolation of the first visit. But I don't know if you'll get what I'm saying, the coast somehow seems made to welcome loads of people. It wants to have people. The second time, it was more "real." What I'm trying to say is that such an expansive, accessible and approachable beach can't be deserted. It doesn't suit its character.

I think that something similar has happened to the island of Serifos. It is not in any way mysterious; it is earthly, simple and clear. The reason why it does not resemble Sifnos and has almost nothing to do with Paros – if we are referring to neighboring islands – is because Serifos keeps some secrets for itself, as well as for travellers. Besides, what's the point if all islands look alike? Fortunately, not one looks like the other. But let's get a little deeper into the essence of Serifos.

I have already talked to you about Livadi, the first settlement you see once you arrive on Serifos. Not bad for a start but there are better things to see. This is the place "for everything" – if you remember the advice at the beginning, you know what this means. There is also Avlomonas beach – a really expansive beach, although no matter how big it is, it is just not big enough. Something a bit more tranquil is needed. Let's make our way the short distance to Livadakia beach. There is sand, several signs of civilization as well as the only campsite on the island (I hope it's still there, check to be sure and not only about this nice campsite, everything in Greece is changing nowadays and not for the better). A short distance beyond the campsite, there is an even better beach – Karavi beach. But of course this is the rule: the further you walk, the more isolated the beaches you will find.

Before we continue to the rest of the beaches, let's pay the necessary visit to Chora, which is one of the three or four most beautiful in the Aegean. It looks like the one in Astypalea and Sifnos (I hope you may see both of them) but still, it has maintained its own style (thoroughly authentic), with gives off the ambience of medieval times, with its narrow cobblestone alleys, tiled roads, ruins of the old castle and mills, which have been rebuilt. Chora is divided into two parts, the Upper and Lower part (Epano & Kato Meria), and offers you a magnificent view of the sea as well as the slight sensation of being hemmed in. Now, you should know two important things about Serifos. First, if you are not keen of walking, you should rent a means of transportation, as I would say that neither the bus nor a taxi is an ideal way of getting around the island. Another important point to note: this island is neither too big nor too small and as such, it accommodates just about as many tourists as it can handle each summer. This is a good thing for the island but not for those who go there during the high season without having made reservations. Don't find yourself in this group; make sure that you have made all necessary reservations in advance. If you go there thinking that you will find a last minute offer, you will most probably end up getting the next ferry home.

Not far from Livadi (if you don't choose to stay there, you will certainly go back), you will find Psili Ammos and Agios Ioannis beaches. You will have to walk to reach the second one. The same rule also applies here: if I were you, I would not stop Psili Ammos at all, I would keep walking, but I may be overemphasizing this point. Even though you will have to walk further, closer to Livadi there are the beaches of Agios Sostis and Lia. During the warmer months, you can reach all beaches of the eastern side by boat. Now, two coasts that I would strongly recommend a visit to are: Koutalas and Chrisi Ammos beaches. Koutalas beach is a large bay in the southern part of the island, close to Megalo Chorio. The beaches (Koutalas, Ganema, Vagia) are exceptional but probably not for typical tourists. On the contrary, one of them is one of the two "official" nudist beaches on the island (the other is Agios Ioannis beach, near Psili Ammos). A short distance from there, you will also find the Castle of Gria and an opportunity to take a short walk. But if you truly want to walk (aside from walking across the whole island, if you are a champion walker that is), you have two main options: the first one is to walk along the waterfront from Livadi to Psili Ammos. The other one is to travel across the inland, starting from Livadi and going up toward Chora. Go for both of them! You will learn many things about Serifos and quite a lot about about the Cyclades and maybe something about yourself!

Sifnos

35

Sifnos

If the islands were a company of fine ladies … pardon me for putting it this way, but I more often fantasize about keeping company with groups of women as this is how I have come to love them, but you are welcome to imagine them as a group of gorgeous men if you like… So, if islands were a group of magical girls, the perfect analogy for Sifnos would be the girl that the teacher would always point out as a role model. Yes, I admit that I get a bit excessive with the metaphors but allow me to say just a little bit more. She, Sifnos, would be the girl that you would notice straightaway. Of course, nothing prevents you from loving another one; perfect analogies and exemplary behaviour do not always herald love. Still, the first impression always counts for a lot, don't you think?

In any case, let me tell you what I think. Sifnos is the first island that comes to mind when you think of the Cyclades. Why's that? Because it's an island that has it all – and in such proportions that really feel drawn toward it. "Metro" (which more or less means harmony, balance), is a magical word created by the ancient Greeks, which seems to have manifested on this island more than in any other place. Consider that Sifnos is the perfect distance away from Piraeus. The journey getting there is neither tiring nor expensive. By the time you arrive, you'll have got the ideal amount of the Aegean breeze. Also, the island has the kind of beaches that create the perfect conditions for your first experience with the Greek sea. Actually, it could – though it ought not – be your one and only experience, and you would still feel that you have already experienced enough. You will have got the basic idea – let's say, the key pieces of the Greek puzzle. But let me continue. Sifnos boasts, if not the most beautiful (which may even be possible), certainly one of the most beautiful Choras of the Aegean. And perhaps the most important detail of all: the Beast has come here but has barely succeeded in doing its basic damage. I should say that Sifnos, unlike many other islands, has managed to impose its terms on the Beast. It appears that the Beast has respected Sifnos. It may sound strange, but just for once, I will admit that its interventions have made the place more receptive to tourists, as well as travellers. Without them, the island would still have more wild and unrefined beauty but people would be less willing to visit Sifnos. So, considering everything in good measure, Sifnos has become more approachable, welcoming and earthy. And you can trust me when I say that this won't bother you at all.

The port is always the first place you see once you arrive at an island. In Sifnos, the port is called Kamares. You will not stick around even if you could, especially if it's not the crazy period around the religious festival which takes place on the 15th of August, as even this area is affected by the festivities. Without doubt, the rest of the year, it has a certain kind of authenticity, especially if you stray from the beautiful beach. But I think you like the difficult stuff. So, you will probably ascend toward the two villages with ancient names: Artemonas and Apollonia (just think that the former has the masculine version of the name for the goddess Artemis, while the second one was built in the honor of god Apollo but was given the feminine version of his name!). Apart from the history, Apollonia – the capital of Sifnos – as well as Artemonas, a short distance away (distances are short in Sifnos; hikers should bear this in mind) only have traces of ancient history, picturesque beauty and Cycladic architecture. However, I believe that the place that will take your breath away is the ancient, medieval capital. I call it Chora (a usual name for the Cyclades) but its real name is Kastro (which means "Castle"). A magical settlement built around a castle, its arrangement at the top of a hill is reminiscent of an amphitheatre. It's easy to understand the logic (and fear) behind this choice of construction. The houses are built really close to each other and arranged in rings, and the most important homes (as it's the always case) are positioned close to the centre of the successive rings. Today, Kastro has no reason to fear anyone, least of all the Beast which has no power here. Kastro offers you an excellent perspective on architecture which was created purely out of human need, which has managed to survive with the passage of time (as well as the passage of fear). It has maintained its beauty and symmetry as a gift to visitors' eyes. Here you can observe the simple, unaffected, functional, symmetrical, totally white settlement which had significance for an entire civilization. It can still teach us many things.

We can now have a look on the beaches. Vathi and Platis Gialos (which means "Wide Seaside," and it is truly wide!) are typical sandy beaches, not totally untouched by the so-called "tourist development" – one cannot have it all. When I first went to Sifnos, everyone told me that I should definitely visit the beach which is near Crysopigi Monastery. I went there and the Monastery is located in a great position (even if visiting monasteries is not my cup of tea) but the beach did not really impress me. I recommend neither Faros nor Apokoftos beaches. I don't think they are awful – not at all. I would like for your delight on this island to be complete, from the Cycladic perspective. I would rather that you take the path from Faros beach which will lead you to Glifos beach. Also, I prefer that you go to the northern part, to the beaches of Cheronissos, Agia Marina, Saoures (despite the rocks) and Vroulidia, but definitely not during the hot season.

You should also know that the paths are just as important (and for some people even more) as the beaches and ideal for helping you get to know the island better. The terrain of Sifnos is perfect for traversing its cobblestoned and earthy paths. What was once a functional design for the difficult, daily needs of the locals, has now become a unique way to experience the Cycladic way of life and enjoy the beauties of the island. Fortunately, the contemporary population of Sifnos followed in the footsteps of the previous generations, something that does not happen often, and they really made the best of their island. Thanks to the path network, the island belongs to Natura 2000, the European network of natural protected areas.

The first time I went there, things were a bit primitive. I mean that we slept in sleeping bags right on the beach right where the ship had left us that night. It was not very comfortable, there were many like us – groups of teenagers who were looking for others to hang out with. It did not go that well for me. I still remember the sweet face of a Danish girl who was staying in the opposite tent. There were three of us and we all tried to chat her up, without success. During the rest of our time, we explored the island by motorbike, with hardly any food eat and lots of adolescent nonsense. The second time, a briefer visit, things were better. I finally managed to get to Chora sober. But the third time was magical; September was coming to an end, the island was free of tourists in a wonderful yet melancholic way. We were alone at the campsite.

It didn't last long, but this is how happiness should be. I hope that campsite is still there. I did go to Sifnos one more time but I was a family man then. So, nothing to add...

You can still go there, even better if it's September, and perfect if you're in love.

Milos,
Klima

Milos

There goes a beautiful island, an island with personality. There goes an island which from a distance seems like an ordinary Cycladic one, but it is not. How can it be ordinary when it hides all this life underneath? This "underground" or even stone life that has offered prosperity to the island thanks to the marbles and other rich deposits of a series of minerals.

Well, there is an element that determines the life and the history of Milos: the mineral resources. For centuries, Milos has lived thanks to the hidden "treasures" within the island. This has given economic self-sufficiency to the island and has kept the Beast away until the last decades. When the self-sufficiency was over, for reasons related to the general mistakes in the economy of this country, Milos sought for the necessary revenues in tourism. Fortunately, it was too late for its "development" as it happened with other islands which exclusively rely on tourism. However, a little piece of evidence of the underground life of the island lies in its catacombs. My first time in the island I was quite lucky to go down there as it was not yet prohibited. Now it is prohibited, but then I was enough coward and claustrophobic not to go on, to crawl to be more exact, more than just a few meters. Today, I cannot even do that anymore. A few years ago, when I returned there, I found the catacombs closed (as a matter of fact, the entrance was "sealed") for reasons that no one cares enough to explain – as thousands of issues that remain inexplicable in this country. At least, the ruins of ancient Milos are still in the area.

But we shall go on even without the catacombs. Milos is rather known because of a wonderful statue, Aphrodite of Milo (Venus de Milo), which ironically, you will never see in the island. You will have to go to the Louvre. Let us return to the island now. There is no space to deal with thieveries of the past. So, how can an island that has a Chivadolimni (Lake of conches) be ordinary? You can still see the lake, maybe a bit tormented, yet you will find it there. And it is not only this. You have the chance to visit a magnificent

"Chora" named Plaka where, if you leave the barbaric entrance aside –if we suppose that you are coming by car or bus (besides there is no other way for you to come), fortunately you are obligated to leave vehicles in a permanently pokey parking (supposedly) space. This is the only way to stroll around the alleys and get in touch with pictures where time seems to have stopped. May the people who built it like this rest in peace; narrow, distant and mystical. Of course, the Beast arrived here as well. But for reasons I explained earlier, it did not stay for long. It satisfied its need for levelling down and rendering everything a tourist attraction and carried on for more durable places.

I love every island but I really care about Milos. It was my first journey, I remember well, with my first beloved girlfriend (God only knows where she is now, over thirty years later, it was the first island I went with my wife (coincidentally, she has the same name as my first girlfriend –it is like the beginning and end of an adventure) and daughter when she was still a baby in the stroller. I really love Milos, but the small village Klima has a special part in my heart and is a place where, all these years, I have dreamt to live in, even for a while.

The entire island lets out a sense of tender abandonment. What do I mean by this? I mean that the image of the past is kept alive, in the two or three towns, Adamas (Diamond, another ironic reminder), Plaka and Apollonia (the land of god Apollo which the locals call Polonia) as well as in the villages, beaches, seacoasts and capes. Let's take the example of Klima in the northwest edge of the large cove of Milos. It is so authentic, precisely because it is just a fishing village left to its destiny. It looks like a stubborn fisherman who insists on fishing with nets when all the rest are occupied with fish farms –or should I say: tourist farms? Klima is there and seems unaffected from the passing of the time. Take a close look at the colours, intense, vivid and blissful without any particular purpose rather than the pleasure of your eyes. Few come in handy regarding the occupancy from tourists and no one for showing off. Look at the small houses; you will find none with more than two floors. And you know why? Because two floors are hardly "useful". The ground floor is mainly used for the boats to have a shelter when the weather does not play any jokes. When there is only sea, sky and several colorful houses. Nothing else. Do we need anything else to feel happy? Yes, a boat. That is why there is the ground floor in the houses in the village of Klima.

Let's also take a look at a few more beaches: Fyriplaka beach in the south, Sarakiniko and Mytakas beaches in the north, Papafragkas beach (the most impressive one) in the east, constitute beaches of rare rocky beauty as well as Kleftiko beach in the southwest (only accessible by boat), while the sandy coast Palaiochori (Old Village) in the south is for more classic taste. Apollonia is a good proposition to those who just want to swim. The village is pretty likeable and gives the chance for a quick excursion –by boat- to Kimolos island, right on the opposite side. The beach in Adamas is nothing special, it is ideal for families that don't like moving around. However, regarding Adamas village, I should certainly mention the museums: the small but exquisite Ecclesiastical Museum (with kind guides) which is set in Adamas as well as the Mining Museum of the island. In Plaka, you should visit the Archeological Museum –it worth the visit just to see the building. Afterwards, you are free to go to one of its nice coffee shops or tavernas and let yourselves to the great endless blue of the Aegean Sea. Keep this sensation forever inside you…

I have to say that I visited Milos two more times after 2013, the first as a family man, and it was ok and the second when our Sand Festival took place in 2018, in Chivadolimni. And it was just perfect!

Syros
The patriarch of rebetiko *(urban Greek folk music in the 1930s)* in Greece was known, as it usual is with all the legends, by his first name, Markos. It all began when he was still a child; he was wandering around the slums of Syros when he had the genius idea to climb on a hill and throw a big stone towards the town, to see what it would

happen. The stone injured another kid, not severely, but little Markos' fear was enough to make him take, the same exact night, the ship to Piraeus. Piraeus was full of lumpen proletariats, refugees of Asia Minor –among them some great self-taught musicians- joints of rebetiko music, khanqahs, cursed and outcast people. Markos' divine gift took charge of the rest and gave birth to a legendary kind of music, rebetiko. But it all began in Syros, in this cosmopolitan island in the heart of Cyclades, and everything was sealed with the rebetiko hymn, Fragkosyriani, dedicated to a woman whose form had never met. She was like a shadow that haunted his life and for her sake, he composed this song; a song about the eternal nostalgia for this ideal woman –and the return to the ideal island.

Little things from the above mentioned are related to Syros of today which still keeps a cosmopolitan air, but is more down-to-earth and more receptive, this is the key word for the island. Certainly, in the history of the island, which was at its peak during the 19th century, after the Greek liberation but also the first half of the 20th century, there are other significant milestones and famous Greeks such as Emmanuel Rhoides, the writer of the satirical and quite scandalous –for the time speaking- epic, "Pope Joan". A more important personality, probably because he is still currently relevant today, is the fabulous lyricist Giorgos Souris, also born and raised in Syros. For years he was publishing a metric satirical newspaper called "Romios" (Greek), while around the same period he was mocking the political affairs in the country. You can still find certain pieces of these, in today's newspapers.

History has also left its signs on the population's composition of Ermoupoli (capital of Cyclades); the strong catholic element –Syros is an island whose life and progress was protected from pirates, as well as the marvelous architectural monuments, churches, neoclassical and stately buildings that proved to be quite resistant to the devastating needs of "progress" and touristic development.

I have travelled many times in Syros looking for the warmth that a serene and receptive friend can offer you. There is nothing passionate to this island (even though I have to admit that once I had sneakily come just to enjoy the company of a group of girls who unfortunately remained just that, company), there is nothing to brag about later to your friends. Still, there is serenity, nostalgia, relaxation (in the alleys of the town while you ascend towards the catholic side, of the "Avgou" (Egg), in the beautiful seacoasts that you can find in a short distance) and one more thing that all sufficient Cycladic islands offer you: they welcome you as traveller instead of hunting you down as tourist. Syros does not pretend to be the picturesque windblown Cycladic island (even though at some points, it still keeps the picturesqueness) nor the island where you are going to make all your wild dreams come true. Syros welcomes you as you are and is given to you as it is.

Except for the casino which has prevailed at the port for the last twenty years, not many things have changed since the beginning of the 80's when I had first visited the island. Some changes are inevitable: more hotels, more noise, more traffic in the streets, overcrowded beaches. On the other hand, some changes are more than welcome: better road network and transport, more frequent connection to Piraeus and other islands –you should consider 6 hours of travel with a normal ship and prefer schedules where Syros is the first disembarking port. Once you are in the island, you can move around by various means of transportation; from mini buses to carriages and from the typical touristic train to boats, your transportation is a matter of choice. For totally plain tastes, the organized beaches (far too much, at least for my taste) Galissas (there is a very nice camping here), Finikas (Palm Tree), Posidonia (della Grazia), Azolimnos, Agathopes (all of them at a short distance from Ermoupoli), and Megas Gialos (Big Bay) in the south. Personally, I prefer the calm Kini beach in the north and a while after that Lotos beach. Of course, a better idea is to catch the boat to Pakou or one of the plenty nudist beaches (and generally beaches of loners): Armeos, Varvarousa,

Amerikanou (of the American), Lia, Marmari and Fokiotrypes (Holes of Seals). In any case, your base will probably be Ermoupoli where you will have the opportunity to have countless walks in both sides of history, the orthodox quarter of Vrontados and especially Vaporia quarter (Ships) and the catholic Ano Syros (Upper Syros). Two mounts, two quarters, two sides of the cosmopolitan history which have coexisted in the island for centuries. The Archeological Museum, the Industrial Museum and Markos Vamvakaris' Museum (if you are lucky enough to find it open) are worthy of your visit. But Syros just like rebetika is more than one sees at the first sight. Like many things in life, you have to dedicate time and interest so as to truly explore and get to know the island. Do that and Syros will recompense you. Syros is the answer to the question if you can create a touristic island by protecting and not destroying its history. I wish some of the neighboring islands would have followed the same path.

Paros

You can say many things about Paros. At the same time, you can say nothing or almost nothing at all. I will try to do the second one. Well, Paros is one of the most touristic islands in Greece. During the summer, it gets packed with thousands of local and foreign holidaymakers. You can find hotels of every sort of amenities, while in the shops whatever you can afford to pay. Naturally, as every island, it has also many beaches. And in summer months all of them are full. Full stop.

Do you want more? All right.

In Paros, not far away from Piraeus, a tourist will find everything that he wishes for. He will find everything, as in any other touristic resort in the world. The only difference is that here, you will find it featuring a Cycladic background. I hope that you will take a look from the balcony of the luxurious hotel when you return from the restaurant or the pool. If you do not take it, just look down when the airplane will be taking off. If you do not even do this, it will be no one's fault that when returning to your homeland, you will hardly remember the name of the island. It doesn't really matter, it could be anyone. Nothing matters and you will be the Tourist of the Year, if not of the Decade. Keep on satisfying the touristic agents. May I talk to the travellers for a while?

Your stay in Parikia, the capital town of Paros, will be the easy solution. I do not recommend this for July and August. But either way, you will be passing by frequently from there. A few decades ago, Naousa was a picturesque fishing village, now it is a busy touristic fishing village. However, if we are talking about fishing villages, you should better go for Alyki (=Salt Lake) or even better Ampelas village. As for the non-coastal villages, I would suggest Agkairia and Dryos while for more mountainous experiences (if we can consider mountainous a village that is set in an altitude of 250m), you should visit Lefkes. My choice is Marpissa, with the ancient name, the castle and the medieval setting; a truly "different world" within the island. I will now mention certain basic sights, beginning from the capital: the church of Ekatontapiliani (One hundred gates), but also the ancient temples, the Asclepeion in the area of Katapoliani, very close you will see the ruins from an ancient temple, the temple of Demetra, the sanctuary of Pithios Apollo and a bit further, Delio –one more temple dedicated to Apollo. Additionally, in Parikia, there are the Venetian Castle and the standard Archeological Museum. For more unique traveling moments, there is the excursion in the ancient cemetery (and at the same time archeological park) in Parikia, the ancient marble quarries in Marathi (much more impressive than it sounds) and at last, also very close to Parikia –something that it is not ruins- Petaloudes (=Butterflies) with real butterflies from May till July.

Let's pick now some beaches as well –fortunately Paros has a lot so you can avoid the crowded Livadia (Fields) and Kaminia beaches, typical family ones near the capital (but you have the ability to take the boat that leads to Martselo or Santa Maria). Kolympithres beach (a quite impressive rocky landscape and relatively quiet) in the northwest, Agioi Anargyroi and Laggeri with its dunes close to Naoussa but even more, Alyki, Ampelas and Dryos in the respective villages are pretty good choices. As far as Antiparos is concerned, I do not have many things to say. It used to be desert and wonderful.

Is Paros the ideal Cycladic island? For many tourists the answer is yes, for others who have my taste, not really (precisely because of the fact that many people like it). Still, it is an island where you can experience a truly Greek summer with its advantages and disadvantages.

Naxos

Naxos

History goes first. There is a sad story about Theseus, an ancient hero who you may have not heard of or not remember of exactly what his achievement were, besides ancient Greece is full of heroes. Maybe the name Minotaur rings a bell a bit more. Fine, let's narrate the story. Theseus kills Minotaur, in reality in this way Athens ceases the sovereignty of the Minoans. Minotaur was a beast. Theseus needed Ariadne's help and love in order to exterminate it. But during the journey back, the beautiful princess of Crete was of no use anymore. So, he left her somewhere in the Aegean Sea. This is how Dionysus found her in Naxos island, although there are other islands that claim her too.

There is a series of family islands in Greece, in all of its island complexes. I am under the impression that Naxos, Ariadne's island, it the most beautiful among these. Of course, if beauty is something subjective, I would rather say "rich", it is a rich island. In every sense –regarding the things it can provide us. Sufficiency, calmness, peacefulness, respect to its history, balance and also something that in most Cycladic islands impossible to encounter: space. Naxos is the largest island in Cyclades Prefecture and in reality, one of the largest ones in Greece. At this point I should also say that Naxos, as the two previously mentioned islands, Syros and Paros are ideal in case you want to visit even more islands. If we consider Santorini among them, then there you have the most "friendly" in transportation standards islands of Cyclades.

Which are the strong points of this island? Let's say what is not good. Naxos enjoys the whole beauty of Cyclades without the negative features that the touristic development of the busy neighboring islands brings along. But certainly this does not happen in every part of the island. Around the Chora of Naxos, the Beast has played its own game. It has converted the site in a relief of Modern Greek ugliness. But only there you will find something like this. Inevitably, you will have to pass from this point in order to enter to the heart of Chora, the Castle, the Portara (Big Door), the Museums, and the archeological site of Grapa. Enter and find the fantastic small pastry shops, bars and tavernas which lie in the inner part of a town tormented from the crazy residential kitsch that unfortunately burdens every provincial town in Greece. However, we try to forget about that, we keep the beautiful side of Chora and we travel throughout the island.

We travel in Castles: the castle of Apalirou in Sagri village, the Apano (Upper) Castle, in Tragea, in Venetian Towers, the Tower of Chimarou and the Tower of Aghias, in archeological sites such as the one in Palaiopyrgos (Old Tower) in Plaka or Dionysus' sanctuary in Livadi (Field). We look for the majestic statues of Kouroi which remain solid (most likely, an accident during their transfer, detain them forever in the island and gave us the opportunity to admire them from close) near Apollonas village in the towering –for Cycladic standards- mountain of Naxos, Za (Jupiter) where there is also the homonymous cave. I should mention the Byzantine Monastery of Fotodotis Christos in Danakos village as well as the Monastery of Panagia Ypsilotera in Galini (Serenity) village. Also, the churches of Panagia Protothroni in Chalki village –the largest one in the island- and the church of Panagia Drosiani in Moni. Later on, I am writing about Apeirathos village (one of the most beautiful villages in Greece). As for the seacoasts, the entire Naxos is an endless coast, I will begin from the shoreline that starts from the capital and extends for about ten kilometers (!) –it is the most typical touristic coastal part of Naxos- with the beaches Aghios Georgios, Aghios Prokopios, Aghia Anna and Plaka. A little further down in the east, we can choose among Vigla (Watchtower), Aliko (Red) and Pyrgaki (Little tower) beaches. In the south you must definitely see Kalantos and right on the opposite side towards the north, the picturesque Lionas beach. A quarter of a century later, there was no camping. Our family vacations took place in a quite dignified hotel in Aghia Anna with a swimming pool and a playground for our little daughter. I visited again Apirathos village, perfect harmony between the visitors and the locals, I climbed high on Za, I reached Moutsouna (which disappointed me once again –fortunately there is

Psili Ammos (Thin Sand) a few kilometers further on) and I saw the sculptures of Kouroi (big sculptures of young men who were sculptured from 7th to 5th centuries bC.).

It was a nice week without a single drop of alcohol, except for the drinks I bought as gifts to my friends. And without a single drop of craziness as well. But one cannot have it all. Naxos –this only matters- has also changed, the only difference is that it looks better now! Unlike me, Naxos has found a way to totally reconcile the past with the present. Ariadne must be proud of her island!

Andros

Andros

There's a real lady that lives fearless of time and waves, in the north top of Cyclades. It stares at Euboea as well as the maternal port of Piraeus and at the same time, I have the impression that it looks down upon the rest of the Cycladic islands. Andros has this right because of the history and the wealthy families that have left their mark there –let alone that it is probably the most "greenish" Cycladic island. But what exactly does Andros offer to the traveller? First of all –thanks to the short distance- it is the perfect island to begin your adventure in the Greek beaches. Nothing is difficult over there. Your transportation will be as easy as finding a place to stay. If you prefer something more traditional, you should go for Chora, while if you cannot resist the temptations of the touristic euphoria, Mpatsi is the place for you. Equally easily you will find the beach that suits you and even easier things to see and do in order to fill your days with experiences and magical pictures –from the Museum of Contemporary Art to the Sariza Springs, the range of impressions that you will carry with you on your way back, is so vast that it will certainly include your preferences, whatever it may be.

Andros has many faces or many different features that form a quite special but specific character. Everything is at your disposal. Andros is large and confident enough to include and embrace many tourists without converting into one more touristic place. This will never happen.

First of all, its history. It begins from the Phoenicians and continues with the prime periods that reach the Hellenistic period. The following fine era for the island comes in the 19th century when thanks to the trade, the bourgeoisie arrives to Naxos, the former captains become ship owners and later on fleet owners. This golden era that lasted for almost a century and left its marks on the personality of the island, delivered the baton to the touristic development, fortunately under certain conditions.

I have an old map of Andros, back from the 80's. Maps were the only thing that for the past thirty years, I have always kept from every island. By now, I have about 70 and

I hope I can get the other 10 that I lack. It is a personal bet to manage to see all Greek islands that have over 200 inhabitants. I am not far away from that goal. The specific map is very simple. In one side, it indicates all the hotels that were in the island back then –there are thirteen. Do you know how many I counted this year in an advertising website? 93! Without doubt, there must be even more.

Gavrio remains slightly unnoticeable, just like the first time I visited it. With quite a few more touristic trinkets that have not ameliorated it at all. Mpatsi, as I will mention later on, is the capital town of the Lazy tourist but the true capital, Chora is a magical town of unique architecture and marvelous mansions. Let's take for example, the building of Kairis Library which hosts the collection of one of the most enlightened Greeks of modern times, Theophilos Kairis (1784-1853, academic and Enlightenment philosopher who died in prison because he insisted on teaching his beliefs). Also, it is full of museums (Archeological, Maritime, Contemporary Art), monuments and archeological sites. But it's not all about Chora. We are talking about the most "greenish" island in Cyclades, so you have to pay a visit to certain villages such as: Apikia, Strapouries (Strapouries – Taxiarchis – Evrouses is one of the plenty routes that you can follow), Messaria and Lamyra (to begin from the ones closest to Chora). The same goes for the excursion to Sariza Springs, Stenies and Menites villages as well as the riverside villages (Andros is a Cycladic island with rivers!) Achla and Syneti (with the characteristic lion heads in Dionysus' springs). These are also two of the best beaches of the eastern side. Vitali, Zorko and Vori are the other beaches in the east (personally I prefer swimming in the west side). More choices in villages: Meliti and Metochi villages in the area of Strapouries. Best beaches: Pisolimionas, Felos, Limanaki in the northwest and Apothikes, Palaiopolis, Plaka and Chalkolimnonas in the west. All of them are sandy and protected from the frequent winds.

My first time in Andros was like fiction. A lugging ship that left us in Gavrio, a bus that departed quickly as we were getting near and was the last one until the following day (do not think that local transport has really changed since then), our tent in the middle of nowhere and the Cycladic wind more hostile than ever. I still remember Korthi, a small village which did not know what tourist means and ourselves in the other side of the enormous beach, completely alone trying clumsily to hold the tent. No luck at all. It is unbelievable how much Korthi has changed. It remains a beautiful bay and enormous beach and at least from away, the village seems picturesque. All the rest, the emptiness, the serenity, and the wilderness of the landscape are now just part of my memories.

I did not really like Andros then. The second time, things had changed. It was spring and it was the first time that I went in an island and stayed in a hotel, although I had been travelling for over ten years. The hotel room normally cost a fortune, but fortunately it was not open yet for the new season. So, prices were friendly, even for my always short capacities. This is how I got to know Mpatsi –something inconceivable for my last visit during my freaky times. And it was nice, I fully reconciled with Andros and I only needed one more trip to truly get acquainted with Chora.

I did it recently and this was the time I really appreciated the beauty of this island and especially the visit at Chora. Years have passed from my first visit but I could say that Andros is keeping this old feeling of something extraordinary even if there were thousand of tourists all around us. That teaches us that the most important thing when you are on an island is with whom you are with!

Tinos

Throughout my childhood, I have always deeply believed that islands were a place of pilgrimage. Something of this awe must have remained later on in my love for the islands. When I was eighteen, out of the blue the islands became one with my quest for love. This didn't last for long but it also left its marks as by the years, it was converted into love for the islands themselves. But I should return to the religious part. My mother always arranged that our journeys would have some sort of religious mission; a votive offering, a visit in a monastery, a miraculous saint had been always reasons for us to travel and this initiation to the supernatural element, together with Aegina, Cephalonia, Zakynthos, Euboea (also an island) was culminated naturally, in Tinos.

Tinos, an island identified now and then in Greeks' conscience with the worship of Panaghia (Holy Mary). Tinos with its majestic church, the miraculous icon, the thousands of candles, the severe icons and the endless lines of believers who like a swarm get there. Tinos, the great comfort of Greek religious people. My mother was going there consistently once a year, at least as long as she had the strength to do so. When she stopped going, this was a sad omen that the ending was approaching.

Every time that I returned there, not for peregrine purposes like during my childhood, I was thinking that it is a bit unfair for the island. Without doubt, it has gained a special tone because of the worshipers; it has received infinite adoration and has given infinite hope. Still, Tinos is something more than that. It seems like a girl who, from her early age, was devoted to religion and she had not the chance to let herself free to the worldly pleasures of life. The kind of pleasures that you, traveller, can experience by travelling in the island, in its villages, gazing at the dovecotes or swimming in the crystal-clear waters. Among these villages, there is a quite special one, as it became a sort of shelter for artists, mainly sculptors. It is homage for the greatest sculptor of modern Greece, Yannoulis Chalepas, an enormous talent with tormented life. But he was not the only great artist that the island had offered. Nikolaos Gyzis, one of the most significant painters as well as the equally important Nikiforos Lytras and the sculptor Dimitrios Filippotes were also born here. There were more, as if somehow, there had to be born praisers of the island's beauty. Tinos is a lovely island, although few people have the chance to realize that. The shadow of the Church (there are a thousand churches in the island!) has certainly great effect on the life of the island, even today that has gained several steady visitors. On the one hand, Tinos has been benefited from this. Here, the hands of the Beast were not free, the limitations –out of respect to faith- were set early and at the same time, they also limited the errors of a merely touristic island. Tinos has never become one of them. That is why it maintained to a great extent an undoubtedly severe but original look. As it is easy for you to understand, Tinos is one of the islands that worth "discovering". Here are few pieces of information that I hope they will convince you to visit

Naturally, to begin from there, you will see Panaghia (Holy Mary) of Tinos, the landmark of the island. It would be better to avoid going on August 15th, day of the Assumption of Mary which belongs to the believers of the Orthodox Church who throng there from every part of Greece. You will also have to see the old Venetian capital Exomvourgo (they call it also Xompourgo) with its castle, the traditional Triantaros, Smardakito for its ideal Cycladic architecture, Ysternia for its view and Volax for its craftsmen. There is as well the village of the artists, Pyrgos, Chalepas' place of birth and also the place where young artists –not exclusively sculptors- carry on the tradition of Tinos.

As for the beaches, I suggest you (according to their distance from Chora) Aghios Fokas, Aghios Markos, Kionia, Pachia Ammos (Thick Sand), Santa Margarita in Potamia village and Yiannaki and Ysternia bays. Also, Livada beach with its white sand in the west.

You will be definitely impressed by the beautiful houses that you meet in every corner of the island, the traditional settlements, the decades of windmills as well as the marvellous dovecotes, monuments of unique folk creation, mainly built during the 18th and 19th century. They are stone buildings and consist of two floors. Ground floor is used as warehouse, while the upper floor as dove birds house. They are principally built on hillside and in a particular angle so as the landing and taking off of the doves to be easier. It is believed that the figures in the external sides attract the doves. They are over 600. I would suggest the area around Tarampados village where there are plenty.

It really worth exploring this island. You will love it –as its doves do.

Mykonos

I have already talked about my first journey to Mykonos. An awkward initiation into the word of adults. My first great frustration was right after adulthood. The myth: everyone can find a girl in Mykonos. The reality: the only thing I found in Mykonos when I was 18 years old was just a different world (of the wealthy people) and the hot sun that burnt me without mercy. The lack of any tolerance to a young, poor and totally inexperienced man as me was a quite bitter lesson that Mykonos taught me in the beginning of the 80's. The island of the winds (there is no truth to this, Mykonos is the island of luxury, there are much more islands of winds – free of charge- in the entire Aegean Sea) was the first one that entered in the map of the international jet set. It was called like this since the 60's and I should have known that. A very small share belongs to the island Hydra -The Boy on a dolphin (1956), was a movie shot there- but in reality they have nothing in common. Hydra remained stately, exclusive and for a few people, the rich or not so rich. Even last year, in a period of crisis, according to the neewspapers there was a party where the guests, in order to have fun and forget their boredom, were throwing lobsters to each other, the same period when thousands of children in Athens were passing out in the schools because of hunger. In 2011 in Mykonos, €150,000,000 (this is just the official figure) were dealt, during the touristic period. This amount of money belonged to those who arrived by the 6,000 airplanes that landed there during those days. Then they say that Greece has no industries…

I haven't stopped resenting Mykonos all these years. We should not blame the island –any island- for people's vanity and arrogance. It is not the island's fault. I returned thirty years later, not to play with lobsters, but to go back to the alleys of the town, take photos of the churches, cast an eye on the beautiful but necessarily blasé women who stay there during summer, pass by the Venetian port. Undoubtedly, I would not choose to live here, even if I could to, but I cannot deny that certain people have invested here and maintained an elegant, luxurious island capital town.

But in Mykonos, it isn't all given in to newly rich ones, although the most dreadful urban developing violations, the most pointless wasted money in ferocious villas, the most provocative newly rich monuments have grown on its body. The Beast has not just come here; the Beast lives here and maybe this is a sort of justice –if there is such thing on this planet. The most shameless rich have created a world which, just like Midas, they are incapable of touching, let alone tasting. When you destroy almost everything just to show off your wealth, you end up looking across the hill the other who has done exactly the same ugly things as you. Still, I cannot ignore the tourist and maybe the traveller's desire to see what precisely Mykonos is. I will say it again: there are parts where the wealth has created a beautiful, if not superficial, setting of good taste. They may have destroyed all the rest but they are still there. And things are definitely calmer and much more humane in the winter.

I don't know what it will happen to Mykonos in the following years. I can't imagine it as an island for travellers of course; consequently there will be always Mykonos, this or another one, for the rich people to find a place to show themselves off. I would be irrational to believe that Mykonos could possibly return to a sort of purity similar to this that characterized the island before the 60's. I just wish for a little more modesty, a little more love to what has remained there and a little more respect to the substantial. As for the rest, there will be always someone who will think that he is in paradise because he saw an illuminated sign called like this and he just came in. But even the stupidest ones at some point realize what happens. A true paradise would never have an illuminated sign on the outside; nor would it charge you €80 for just an umbrella under the sun.

If I return to Mykonos (actually I've been there quite recently, for few hours –just because I wanted to see Delos and wait for the boat to come), I would only do five things, during the day –I would not stay for the night. Early in the morning, I would stroll around the city, pass by the alleys, gaze at the windmills and later I would have a coffee in Small Venice. Then, I would take the ship to Elia. I would return in the noon and have a quick trip in the north side, in the beaches of Panormos and Aghios Sostis. I would go back in Chora in the afternoon, stop first in the Monastery in Palaiocastro (Old Castle) and by the evening, just before departing, I would ascend to the small headland near the church of Aghi Anargyroi and gaze at the sea. This would be all that I would do −but (not for all the treasures of Mykonos) not in July or August. This would be enough for me. Goodbye Mykonos. As far as I am concerned you are just a stop before Delos. This is how it should be.

Delos

Delos

A sacred island where is forbidden to touch anything. Most importantly, the shadow of the ancient ancestors. So close to Mykonos, isn't it really ironic? Not at all, if we consider that everything began there. Delos is the center; the ancient queen while the rest of the princesses were gathered around her. Delos was the center. Remember: Cyclades derive from the word κύκλος (cycle). In reality: around Delos.

What was so special about this island and could have gathered so much respect? On the one hand, the more essential depiction of the power of Ancient Greece (if we said Athens, we would be more correct though). On the other hand, the clearer reflection of an economic colossus, the prime and decline, of course. In its glory days, Delos was the ancient Switzerland where the wealth of the Athenian Empire was accumulated. The luxury combined with the fear for the sacred treasures got close to madness; no one could be born or die in Delos. The beginning and ending of life were banned here. One more element of the myth –in any case, almost everything was myth back then.

The sanctity followed but the selection was not random. At it's peak, this island had 30,000 inhabitants. It is impossible to imagine something like that today when just a large group of tourists seems like a crowd among the ruins of the ancient temples, the statues, the columns which have fallen in the ground, the famous lions. The lions… In my opinion, the story of the lions is the most ironic description of Ancient (and mainly modern, alas) Greece and every other transient empire. In the beginning, they were placed in the entrance of the island so as to make the visitors feel awe. Later on, when the power was just a memory, they were transferred in the inner part of the island. No one was afraid of Delos' lions anymore. They were only there to amuse the passersby. They were not guarding anything else rather than the memories of the greatness that was lost in time.

However, what else can we find in Delos today? In a few words, it is the perfect place for you to feel the spirit of ancient times. Except for the humble buildings of the museum and the smaller ones which were used by the archaeologists and the permanent guards, there is nothing else rather than memories of that glory. Still, sanctity imposes even today its own rules. The island does not accept tourists −not in the way that they intrude to the rest of the islands. Delos, unreachable, proud and lonely, has kept all glory for itself. Even today, this place welcomes you only just as pilgrim. The only difference is that there are no wealthy locals.

I visited Delos old enough to have many illusions − neither for the island nor for myself. I tried to see as many ancient monuments as I could and principally to feel the atmosphere of the glamour of the past. A polite employee of the museum, named Yannis helped me a lot to this purpose. They say that it is hard to find a public worker in Greece who loves his job; and even harder to love and also know it well. Still, sometimes it happens. This man −the joy of feeling useful by talking to someone about the beloved ancient world was marked on his face, helped me understand much more than the anaemic −bonus- map given in the entry together with the relatively cheap ticket or the information of the guides who flood the island in various languages. He helped me understand the importance of respecting the sacred site. This man has also given me a map, a real map which I lost later when I was running over the ancient stones in order to catch the disembarking ship. Was it a sign to come back? I took it that way.

In any case, I had already learnt a lot. I entered to the Sacred Town whose history began 3,500 years ago, I saw my reflection in the Sacred Lake, I passed from the place where Apollo was born, I traversed the Markets (Agora) of the Delians, the Kompetaliasts and the Italians (each one constitutes a symbol of a different era), I saw the House of Dionysus, the House of Hermes, I tried to make out, as much as I could (admission is prohibited) the House of the Masks and the House of the Dolphins, I saw the Sanctuary of Hera as well as the Sanctuary of Zeus and Heracles, I stood before the Stadium and of course, I spent some time in the Museum. I also saw some proud peacocks wander among the ancient ruins. I spent several hours walking in Delos, although my secret desire was to spend the night there. How ironic is the fact that the ship leaves and leads you almost mandatorily to Mykonos? The sensation, after having lost yourself for some time in the shadows of the past, makes the comparison terrifying. But it's not Mykonos' fault. If there is someone to blame, this is the times that keep changing. I will return again to Delos, I promised it to myself and I will do it. This is not an island to jest with.

Santorini

I could say a lot about Santorini. I will try to stick to the basics -my own basics. I have been to Santorini in every season and in every note of the love stave, if I can call it that way. In my four journeys, I was quite in love, crazy in love, barely in love (imagine, it was the same woman of the second journey) and the fourth time, married. So, I had the chance to see the island in every phase.

It goes without saying that Santorini is a rather touristic island; a multi-filmed island; an island ideal for cruise tourists. A rich island −and an island for the rich, fortunately not just for them. Because at the same time, it is an island that keeps its magic and mystery. Not like before, but it does. Thirty years ago, when I first went there, there was just magic and mystery. You have probably heard about that horrible story with the volcano and the earthquake −the most terrifying earthquake ever during the ancient times. The earthquake formed the geomorphy of the island in a completely different way. Now, about the volcano, if you pay close attention, you might see it still emitting smoke but fortunately, it is harmless.

During my first time, there were quite few hotels, few tourists, many donkeys and the back pebbled beaches had an evocative effect on the visitor. Besides, they were beaches with one or two coffee shops and taverns at all. Today, there are many hotels and few donkeys, mostly as a touch of nostalgia. But the beaches are still beautiful and the sunset in Oia is equally gorgeous −the only difference is that now there are people who think that they have to applaud it! Thirty years ago, no one bothered to applaud the natural beauty of Santorini. The beauty was simply there. And it was an island where it was hard for the locals to get by, especially the first post-war years. The magnificent village of "Marinatos", it was called like this because of the archaeologist who made the excavations in Akrotiri (Cape), was there during my first visit as well. It also faced difficulties, it was shut down in a painful way because of a tragic event, but it opened again recently, safer than ever. As for the modern settlements, they got bigger in a way that you feel that they exceeded the measure. Still, things are not that bad.

If you have to come to Santorini in summer, there are some things I could suggest you should do, but not many. I have already explained that Santorini is one of the most convenient islands to move around and see many other islands. You can go nearly everywhere from here while among other things, it is a "step" to get to Crete. Let's stay to the island though. Things like the volcano, sunset, emerald waters, black pebbles, white architectural notes (at least from far away) which balance on the fine ridge, cinematographic atmosphere, "kanaves" (the old grape-pressings) and wine testing (most varieties, I prefer the white wine, are exceptional but don't overdo it, I have seen many people staggering in the daylight), all these are great and naturally quite expensive (except for Perissa) but maybe the following summer the shop owners will have got reasonable due to the crisis. These are the basics but you should add a visit to Ancient Thira, swim in Finikia in the north side or in Vlychada right in the opposing side in the south, an excursion to the small island Thirasia (the other face of Santorini) and an alternative solution regarding the sunset, a walk to Mpaxedes while the rest applaud the sunset in Oia.

According to my opinion, and I fully recommend it, the perfect time to visit Santorini is spring. If summer belongs to the rich, spring belongs to everyone and especially to the travellers; when tourist invasion is tolerable, the shopkeepers still live in more humane rhythms –this has consequences on the guests, trust me, the decoys do not flock to the port to get clients. Also, sun does not burn mercilessly the black pebbles in Perissa and Kamari. Kamari… Do you have any idea what this word means in Greek? It may be just a name for the place but I like to think that it corresponds to the homophone Greek word: something to be proud of; your favourite. Undoubtedly it is my favourite, I just have to imagine how it was back then; strange, almost deserted and without any scratch from the

Beast. But as we have already said, a lot of time has passed since you necessarily needed the donkeys.

And there's something you must know about the donkeys: many people complaining nowadays about the locals who are torturing the poor animals. Believe me, it is true!

That's the dark side of a famous picturesque island and at least this guide has to say something about it! Just walk up the steps by yourself please!

Ios

There's the bet: I could talk to you about Ios as much time as I need to smoke a cigarette –a normal one, don't get too excited. The bet is based on whether I can be so quick, clear and descriptive to be able to verbalize in such short time letting you know all you need about Ios. I cannot become young again –this is why I haven't been there for many years. But the island doesn't change; it remains unaltered –an island for the youth. Besides, let's play with words, the island is also commonly called "Nios" which means "young" in Greek!

Every new generation of young people in Athens has the delight to discover Ios in the summertime and they have also the naivete to believe that they are the first youngsters to do so. I do know it because I thought the same in the beginning of the 80's, when I went there along with my first girlfriend. This island is made for me, I thought. And I was right, just as thousands of others who every summer believe the same. Ios is Dorian Grey's Cycladic portrait. It is gifted to look always young, always ready to welcome the "freshest blood" who feels that the urban neighbours of Athens and other European cities suffocate them. And the ship that leads them is almost one-way. If you are young you have to discover Ios. If you haven't done this, then something is wrong. Something is wrong with you. This gift and pilgrimage of the young people to youth reflection, permits Ios to put on every few years and a different face and in some kind of way, it preserves all of them until today. It was the hippy face which came in during the 70's, the wild punk one that appeared –together with some new wave faces in the 80's, the more sophisticated –freak style of the 90's, the techno-freak of the 21st century and goes on. So, among all those who come every year for the first time, you will also find the unrepentantly young, who either kept their old-fashioned style either got lost in the blender of periods and masks. But I'd better talk about island stuff before this text ends up being a sociological analysis. Ios has a magical beach, Mylopotas. I think that its heart beats there, a hippy heart derived from the best dreams of the

60's which of course remained dreams. Mylopotas is Ios' heart because this hippy aura has embraced all versions of modern –and unfortunately all clumsy steps of the Beast. Yes, indeed, few things remind of Mylopotas that I saw, in my juvenile eyes there was nothing more close to the sixties and hippy era than the solely café-pub-tavern-whateveryouwant that was lying in the edge of an enormous beach. Under the reed roof, I dreamt of Frisco, Woodstock and the summer of love. These were my dreams about a period that I never lived in. in the lapse of time, dreams, illusions, delusions and constructive crimes were mixed up in the blender of the lifestyle of every time and now, it is just another whatever-you-want beach. The difference is that now it is not just you, but thousands of people, who look for something and whenever so many people look for something in a small place no one finds it, that's a rule.

There is another side of Ios. Of course there is. Every summer Chora is bursting of life, as the proper guides would say. The ports are still there. The beaches are still there. The hostile, for the profane ones, Cycladic wind still blows there; and cools the soul of those who are or insist on being young.

I recommend you Klima, a beautiful beach in the road to Mylopotas in the south. There, you will also find Tris Klisies (Three Churches), not one but three marvellous beaches. Still, in Maganari (I had gone there by boat), there are four and are amazing. In the north, you will see Homer's Grave (it is not the only one, you can find one also in Chios) but I suggest the beaches Psathi and Theodotis while in the east, among other things, you will find Palaiocastro.

I remember several things of my first visit and hardly anything of my second one. From the first one, I remember of a legendary –for the time speaking- bar that you could listen to classical (if it's possible) music and we were calmly having our drinks sat on the stone steps that reminded of an ancient theatre. I remember of the painter Kant with his surrealistic landscapes. I have still one of his paintings –in a postcard, my allowance did not permit me to go further than that. I remember the totally communal sleep in the beach under the frowning faces of the locals. I remember that half of my friends had been robbed by the end of the journey. This was maybe another way of communal life, although quite few of the victims thought of it like this.

From my second visit I just remember a few lazy days in Chora and the calm sea beyond us. I am afraid that my second visit was no more than an omen that my next visit in the islands would only be in the not so near future: Nothing really important to mention.

Sikinos

Is it the most ignored one among the Cycladic ladies? Is it probably, for this reason, the most authentic one? I am not sure of neither, but they are both close to the truth. It is also true that I will never forget my first visit there, with a small ship, a big boat if I recollect well, from Ios or Folegandros. The Chora of Sikinos is a bit far from the port of Alopronia – it is called like this and it means Sea (Αλς-) and Welfare (Πρόνοια). Back then, in 1981-82, we had to choose between the donkey and the sole existing vehicle –some kind of taxi. And in spite of the fact that we had chosen to stay in the beach, Chora came to us out of the blue. We were astonished by watching a quite angry crowd of twenty-thirty rather raging locals who were looking for the nudists in a nearby, totally isolated beach. In the foreground, there was, as always happens at these cases, the priest of the village. They didn't find them in the end, the nudists were clever enough to disappear or at least they put some clothes on, so the protestors returned without success to their Chora. But this incident was marked on my memory as a typical example of the stubbornness that during those years was as frequent as the wind in the small islands of the Aegean Sea.

I was never too in favour or too against nudism but without doubt, this is not the best way to stay pure: chasing nudists in the other side of the island.

In any case, Sikinos one way or another, remained pure. The Beast was never keen on conquering this island. Certainly, the terrible behaviour of the Greek authorities regarding the ship schedules, played its part on that. Indicatively, I should mention that in 2012, during summer, the most fertile months for tourism, there was no ship for the island from/to Piraeus, from Saturday till Monday, that is to say the days when it is most likely for someone to come (or leave) from the island. The general situation of the country is everything but supportive -on this issue- for the future of the island and is a matter of life for Sikinos. Let it be. With or without the ministry bureaucrats, Sikinos has many things to offer to the traveller and trust me, now no one wants to pursue nobody. With or without clothes, you are welcome there.

The inauguration of Pantochara in the island was an important event for the summer of 2011. And I think that it worth the trouble saying a couple of words about it. First that you can find here a very small church of Panagia Pantochara (Holy Mother of Eternal Joy) dedicated to the memory of the great poet Odysseas Elytis. It was one of his last dreams. If you enjoy walking –as happens to most real travellers- you are in the correct place. Once you look at the island for the very first time, you just cannot imagine how many surprises it may hide. The basics consist of walking from Kastro (Castle) to Alopronia and backwards (once, this used to happened, wanting or not), from Kastro to Malta beach or just from Kastro to Episkopi and -backwards. Additionally, the Monastery – fortress of Zoodochou Pigis. It is true that in this part, the local authorities have acted wisely. They have been adjusted to the abandonment conditions from part of the state and they have stuck to the point –the authenticity of the nature of their land; that is why they have promoted the trekking tourism. It is a good choice. Just as the beautiful, lonely (according to the inventory of 2011, the municipality of Sikinos is included among the ten most sparsely populated ones in Greece) full of low Cycladic notes, Sikinos. If the rest leave Sikinos aside is because they don't know it. You shouldn't make the same mistake.

Folegandros

The early years when I was traveling around the islands of the Aegean Sea, I dreamt many times of getting a house in Folegandros. Naturally, this was not a dream about Folegandros only. I have thought of the same thing for at least half of the islands of the Aegean –the fact that I barely had the money to get and stay to the island for just a few days, was another issue. However, especially in Folegandros not only had I detected the right spot, Chora of course, and more specifically the sheer side towards the east Aegean, but I had also found one or two deserted – back then- houses that seemed ideal for sheltering my island life.

I don't have this dream anymore. Like many other, I had to leave it behind. Besides, the important isn't how many dreams you leave behind but how many you will keep with you. Still, this matter is something that I don't think about anymore. It may be Folegandros' fault; not precisely itself but the Beast –in a more sophisticated version- which has come out and walked upon the once unfriendly land. Folegandros, even the name has something magical, it sounds like lyrics, used to be a magnificent island. Now it is just a beautiful island; full of visitors whose majority shows total respect. Still, full of them especially during high season. The once peaceful Chora finds difficulty in hosting all those people who come seeking for uniqueness and special vacations. As it happens when many people, of the same more or less dream, are gathered, no one stays completely satisfied.

I cannot remember many things of my first visit there. It was over thirty years ago but it could have been fifty years ago as well. I mean that the conditions between the 60's - 80's had barely changed. Just imagine that I arrived to the island with the help of a boat which anchored next to the ship and carried the few passengers. It was not an oddity of mine or some local touristic attraction. It was only the fact that there was no port to accept a ship. We were a good company back then, I totally liked two of the girls but as it happens most of the times (I mean with me), I was satisfied with just one –and only for a while. There was no way to get to Chora from the first day. I don't remember if there was even a bus. If there was one, it was too peaky in its schedules. So, we stayed in the beach of the island and spent the night there. I can still see locals' frown faces. We should not take it personally. They just did not want nor know what exactly a tourist means. Still, they were a little more polite with us, just because we were Greeks. What they felt about the foreigners wasn't hostility but fear. And they certainly didn't like the fact that we were sleeping and hugging –to be honest even more than this- right outside their homes and among their boats. A lot of time has passed since then. The next time I went there, some fifteen years afterwards and quite in love with a blond lady, it was impossible to detect the small houses of the first time. What we did found easily was a very friendly hotel of Cycladic architecture, view to the sea and all amenities that a lazy tourist needs. There were at least ten similar ones which were springing up from every side of the beach. But this was the less important. In Chora which I had adored the first time because of its authenticity, I found hundreds of Athenians who had also come in search of the (lost) authenticity. No, it was not nice. The coffee shops were carefully set, the square was marvellous, the taverns were likeable, the beauty of the Aegean all around, everything was at its position. But somehow It was not the same. Fortunately, we randomly met a very sweet couple who ran a local shop in Karavostasis beach and they led us to a relatively isolated village in the north of the island, where the paved road was ending. It was there where authenticity had found shelter. But I should be fair and say that Folegandros, for someone who gets to know the island now and doesn't carry any useless memories but only his sunblock, iPad and credit cards, constitutes a very comfortable way to experience the Cycladic atmosphere. Both times I tried but didn't make it to Chrysospilia (Golden Cave). It is only accessible by the sea but still, if you get until there, they won't let you go in. So, there is no point. But we shouldn't want it all. The church of Panaghia (Holy

Mary) is always there, standing high over Chora; the promenade till there, the entire landscape and the view, is something you have to experience. The proud Kastro (Castle) of Chora is still there. Katergo, the magical beach – you also need a boat to reach it, unless you are willing to walk a lot- is also there, the same stands for Livadaki beach. A third choice is the "greenish" beach, Vorina, also requires a boat. The most famous beach is Agali (Embrace), however the second time it didn't impress me at all. But Folegandros has one more key-factor. Chora may have become the "authentic" game of the Athenians, but all the rest of the parts of the island are completely untouched by the Beast. Consequently, you can fearlessly seek the real Cycladic beauty there. You will just be a bit crowded in your way there.

Koufonissi

MINOR CYCLADES
Koufonissi (Pano)

It is impossible to think of Koufonissi without thinking of colours. Unlike other islands whose palette of colours is limited, the blue of the sea, the white of the houses, chapels and windmills, the yellow of the void fields and wind, Koufonissi fascinate you by it's colour. There are two islands, Pano (Upper) and Kato (Lower). Here we are going to refer to Pano Koufonisi - which has been inhabited since the prehistoric era.

If paradise were an island, according to text of the map which I have kept from my first visit there, *it would be in the Aegean Sea and it would be called Koufonissia.* No objections to that, but my own paradise would include all the beloved islands.

In Koufonissi, the first thing that enchants you is the light green beach that welcomes you, I wonder if it is still the same –I haven't been there for several years and I miss it. Green and blue are met and mixed up in every version in the beaches of the island. But I don't have just sea in mind when I talk of colours; I mostly talk of the wonderful colours of the houses in the of the port. There are times when you compromise even with the Beast. Still, here the Beast was just a simple kitten before the wittiness of the locals who –a rare thing for the Greek standards- made their island more receptive to tourists without altering it. At least, this is how it looks to my eyes. I enjoyed of all these colours, these well-preserved houses when I went, once before and once more after the small love explosion by principally, the Athenians. All these happened back in the 90's and by the youngsters Greek tourists (mainly from Athens) who claimed their own sophisticated paradise in Koufonissia. For about two, three or four years, it has remained a secret which was spread over from friend to friend, later it became a mutual secret and finally a classic route in the Aegean Sea. However, Koufonissia lasted, exactly at the point when they were about to have the luck of Adam and Eve's paradise –to be lost from everyone and forever- and kept the most important thing of all: their colour. In Greek, I don't know if the same happens with other languages, when we say that a place keeps its own colour, means that it keeps its own identity, truth and in the end, the authenticity. Nowhere else this is more literal rather than Koufonissia.

The first time there it was a bit of adventure, and my love story that was connected to the colours of the island, equally intense and magical. Imagine: very little money, we were sleeping (almost not all) in the sand, next to the camping (if one could call it a camping) to take advantage of its facilities with small intrusions during the night and without paying a penny. Am I ashamed of that? Not really. It was part of my personal mythology (traveling without paying, sleeping without paying and from time to time, eating without paying –but I won't give any advice on this matter here), that I don't have any intention of denying.

In contrast to my typical advice that I give in the beginning, in Koufonissi there is a port where you can swim. Still, this is only the beginning. Just see the beaches and decide on your own. Platia Pounta and Charokopos are ideal for the Lazy Tourist, if he bothers to get till there. But Pori is even better... The truth is that the beach of Italida (the Italian lady) disappointed me a bit, I expected something more magical but the way till there was a very nice experience. All beaches are accessible on foot –it's always the best way to get to know an island. It goes without saying that you will take the boat that leads to Kato Koufonissi (especially in the celebration of August 15th) and also to the deserted Keros, a significant Cycladic center of Ancient times.

As for my second journey there, I just enjoyed of Koufonissia. Only Italida beach seemed very small or very crowded. Apart from this It was like meeting an old friend. It's the same feeling. It is less intense but it lasts more.

Kato Koufonissi
A few hundred metres from Koufonissi there is a small island with the same name – only accompanied with the adverb Kato (meaning lower, downside). This is an island without permanent inhabitants – but full of brave young

tourists in the summer. There are not many options here. In the daytime you can walk or swim. In the night you can either sleep in a sleeping bag or a tent or catch the small boat for Koufonissi island. I think the last boat from Kato Koufonissi departures at 21:00 o'clock –but you know that these timetables can change every year. The boat from Koufonissi stops first at *Panagia* – (Virgin Mary: Once a village but now just a settlement of few little houses) and then on the beach *Nero* (water). Nero is a beautiful beach but I preferred to spend a few hours at the Panagia place. You can walk from there and find another beach in a relatively short distance. I can't remember the name of the beach but, trust me, it is difficult to miss a place you search for in Kato Koufonissi. The acreage of the island is just 4,3 sq.Kms!

It was night when we reached the island, it was the second night of our Sand Festival in 2016 (you may read more about it at the end of the book) and I loved the place, it was the happiest moment of our festival that year. I also loved the atmosphere and the food at the tavern "Venetsanos" (opens only in the summer). You know I don't usually write about taverns, hotels, e.t.c. but it wasn't just a tavern, it was a kind of time-machine.

If you ever go to Koufonissi, don't forget to visit Kato Koufonissi… You must see this -one of a kind- island!

Iraklia

If you have noticed it, we are in Minor Cyclades; a small group of islands, a small circle within the big one. Small is beautiful. Not always but in this case for sure. Iraklia –just 19 square kilometres- is probably too small for your taste. No large beaches, no large hotels, not even large pools. On the contrary: big portions of freedom, of spaciousness, the biggest portion of serenity you will ever find. Iraklia is a miniature painting in pastel shades of blue. Like all tiny paintings, require extra attention to detail –still, is a work of (traveling) art. And such one, it worth your full attention. Access to Iraklia and generally to small Cyclades is an issue. During the hard months of winter, ships ditch the island. One route till here per week, or two (alas, some weeks there is not even one) and a few more in the summer. A legend of Minor Cyclades comes to fill in this gap; the ship –together with the captain from whom it was named by- Skopelitis. It sails through Minor Cyclades and permits the communication with the "large" ports, Paros, Naxos, Amorgos, consequently with the rest of the world. No one knows for sure when it started the schedules –it doesn't really matter after all. What does matter is that it exists –at least it existed last year-and I hope forever, like every legend. Something like the Flying Dutchman in a milder version –and always in microscale.

Once, this island was called Gaidouri (Donkey). They say that it was called like this because of its shape. The truth is that by looking the tiny map that I had brought from there, I cannot find any similarities. But if we are talking about an easygoing creature, patient with your (though few) demands and willing to… travel you, then yes, it matches. The microcosm of Iraklia has everything that a traveller would want but nothing for the Lazy tourist. It is not coincidence that you always meet strange people there. It welcomes you –so to speak, because nobody won't be interested in selling you something as happens elsewhere- a tiny settlement, Aghios Georgios, few houses and one café-tavern with a long and narrow table and in the middle (of the table) there is an impressive… tree. This is the first settlement, there is only one more. The village of Panagia is not far away. Nothing is far away from you in Iraklia. The beaches are literally at your feet. The cave of Aghios Ioannis which is located in the bottom of the sole mountain, called Papas, is one of the most beautiful of the Aegean as well as a reason to traverse the inland and climb to its top. The route begins from the settlement of Panagia. Also, in Livadi bay, there are the ruins of a Kastro (Castle), the entire area is called like that, where there were sanctuaries devoted to god Zeus and goddess Tychi (Luck). But if you have come to Iraklia, you are… lucky either way.

Schinoussa

Is this my favourite island? In any case, it is the one I think of when I am down. In a few words: someone comes and says, *"You know, Gregory, I've got bad news. You are prohibited to go to all Greek islands* (everything is possible in this country, the sentimental journeys may become a criminal offense). *Except for one. You may choose. Choose now"*. The answer is: *Schinoussa*. Why? I have plenty of reasons.

First of all, I loved Schinoussa because it was an island that I walk every inch of it. How they call it: the world in your pocket? Well, this island was in my pocket. And I didn't care at all about the rest of the world. I was in love back then. But the love that did last was the one for the island. I don't know if there is anything more beautiful in the Aegean sea, or generally in life rather than waking up in a small, humble totally white house of dark blue windows, watching infinite small fields around you and further down, your own, infinite sea. I don't know if there is anything more beautiful rather than being healthy and in a great mood, starting your day by thinking of "your" beach for the day, a small sandy beach. Then you walk till there, enjoy the sun and sea, play in the sand without any disturbances. I am never disturbed by two, three, five even ten people who enjoy, equally peacefully, of the sea, who respect the landscape and share with you this emotion that ends up getting a bit metaphysical, even if you have never had this sort of tendencies before.

And later, when the sun is right above you, your mood changes and you want something else, also special, once again on your own feet and nothing else, in the pace of your walking, accompanied by the Cycladic breeze. You traverse the dirt road among dry stones and you go to something else, similar but still so different, a paradise shelter.

And later, you meet the same people. You cannot and you don't want to do otherwise. Two or three taverns in the port, Mersini, two three more in the village of Schinoussa called Panagia. A grocery, literally like the old times, the little store where you could find everything, (or you thought you could because you were just a child); and a coffee shop that looks at the sea when the sun rests; and a friendly bar, maybe two or three more where you can listen to the music you like when you are having your drink, before you return to the totally white house with the dark blue windows. And if you share your bed with the person you're in love with, you have more than you could ever expect in this life.

You have everything.

There is one more small village, called Messaria and (you've known that already from the rest of the islands) the name means that it is set in the middle of the island and in most of the occasions is like that. Here, it is set in the northern side but this kind of information doesn't really matter. You can see the entire island at your ease, within a few hours. If you are a traveller, these hours will be some of the most beloved ones that you have passed in the Aegean. I will now mention some beaches: Tsigkouri, the closest one to Panagia village, the beach of Liolios, the most touristic (this seems a joke when you are in Schinoussa), Alygaria and Psili Ammos (my favorite one) and Fountana (which I also like although it hasn't the spaciousness of the rest). The handmade map that I have (in a photocopy) mentions 15 beaches, there may be more, it doesn't matter. Besides, you will see them all!

Days go by in a way that reminds of sweet routine but it's something more than that, an initiation to simplicity and also to completeness. To the small and majestic. Elytis, the poet (Nobel prize in Literature, 1979), says that better: *this world, the small, the great!* These are some of the most famous lyrics by the poet who worshiped the Aegean Sea and they could, in my opinion, have been written about Schinoussa), dedicated to the white and all together to the entire fan of colours.

As days go by, you meet people and they meet you, you get the illusion of familiarity with a place and a landscape that practically don't belong to you but substantially are yours.

I don't know, traveller, if all these have convinced you. If not, you can sail for the next island. I have already done everything I could to persuade you to fall for Schinoussa. Small, humble, almost invisible, -fortunately- for most people, it is just waiting for you (and me).

EAST CYCLADES
Astypalea

"This is an island for couples!" I said the first night of my journey there, in another friendly camping, full of couples – of course. We were very young –for Greeks, camping is a matter of the young ones, the older modern Greeks used to do (and unfortunately plenty of them keep on doing) something like camping, usually exactly in places where they shouldn't camp at all, carrying together all their domestic equipment except for the roof and the walls.

Which was my problem? Reasonably speaking, I shouldn't have one. I was perfectly tuned with the environment: it was a journey in Astypalea with the girl I had a long-lasting relationship with. I had no problem at all. I just missed my friends. And the opportunity of creating exceptional memories. This was another thing, this was only my problem. All the rest were satisfied. Or at least they seemed so. So, there were couples everywhere who enjoyed their vacations and the idyllic phase of their love, the point you need just your partner, the sky, a camping and an island that provides you the basics. Astypalea surely provides these basics. From this point, it is a secure island. It seems like it knows all the right answers in the hypothetical test for the acquisition of the island identity. Does it have beaches? Yes. Does it have a picturesque Chora? Yes. Does Chora have a Castle? Yes. Does it have a satisfactory road network? Yes. Does it have nice hotels, camping, pensions, restaurants, taverns, cafes, bars? Yes, yes, yes, yes. Well, then why have I not adored Astypalea? Probably because of that. I didn't find anything unusual, bizarre or extreme, anything that didn't match there. Everything is at its position like the breakfast of a neat pension. Everything is simple, easily accessible, summery and sunny.

Some necessary information: you will not stay for long in Pera Gialos, the port of your disembarking. Naturally, you will ascend to Chora (it is one of the most beautiful Chora's of Aegean Sea – just like a postcard with it's Venetian Castle. Further down, there is a line of beaches, all with the same name, Marmari (Marble). These ones as well as Livadi beach, in the opposite side but always in a short distance from Chora and Maltezana (Assumption) beach have the pros and cons of a touristic beach. You should better reach Aghios Ioannis (in the southwest side of this strangely shaped island). In your way there, you will also find the path to the Monastery of Panagia Vlefariotissa. I also think that the excursion to Mesa and Exo Vathi (=Inside and Outside) worth the effort. Not so much for the sea but because you find yourself little further from the wild crowd of the hot season. There are certainly excursions by boat –I believe that it is the most fascinating thing you can do, given that even the amusement in the island keeps a low profile- to the nearby islets such as Ophioussa (Female Snake), Pontikoussa (Female Mouse) and Chondro Nisi (Fat Island).

   Do you want to have vacations by the book (not this one, the other books)? Do you want to proceed by following the instructions? Do you want to be certain of your every step? In your way out, do you want to fill in the notebook of the hotel or the registration of the respective website with plenty of stars and comments such as: It was really beautiful, we will definitely come back? Astypalea is waiting for you. It is there to fulfil all your reasonable desires. In my case, I visited the island only that time. But I never claimed to be the role model for proper vacations.

*One more thing. Technically, Astypalea belongs to Dodecanese. But not in this guide. Here it goes like the route of a traveller

Amorgos

It is certain that this is a much publicized island. It is even more certain that this film (The Big Blue by Luc Besson) attracted many people to Amorgos, often for the wrong reasons. But Amorgos that I loved since not only myself but also the island –touristically speaking- were still young, is a wonderful island that worth visiting. Even if you get there for the wrong reasons.

In Greece, I assume in other countries as well, since the beginning of the 90's, Amorgos was widely known because of its famous vibes. I have never selected an island because someone told me that it has *great vibes*. Let's say that it does have. I am not an expert. But if it is so, then they also do half of the islands that I have written about in here. For me, an island worth visiting for other reasons which are visible just with our beautiful eyes. Our soul follows -but this is another story.

In any case, my soul enjoyed the island most during the first visit, in the beginning of the 80's rather than in the following ones. There were many isolated beaches, there was the unbelievable distance –at least technically as there was no road- between its two main ports, there were too many strange places for you to explore it but still, everything was more innocent and authentic. I still remember of the groups of friends that were formed in the beach, boys and girls who gathered to listen to the music around the fire, the hipsters who laid their sleeping bags in the beach and in the almost non-existent camping –it was just an empty land with a few tormented trees.

It was then when I first saw Chora and I still recollect of how difficult it was for my bike which could not stand the uphill and left me go on, together with my girlfriend –she was my first girlfriend-, on foot till the top while the temperature was over 40 °C. I was recompensed as I met the most beautiful Chora of the Aegean. I remembered of the poet Nikos Gatsos and I think I understood why he compiled just one poetry collection (it was considered very important for the time speaking) named "Amorgos" and no other poems afterwards but only lyrics for songs. Chora is an enchanting symphony of white with some touches of the rest of the colours. Naturally, I bowed before the beauty of the landscape around the Monastery of Chozoviotissa (you can see the photo I took then) as well as the nearby small rocky coasts. Then I returned (again by ship!) to Aegiali – Katapola is a rather ordinary island village for you to stay there. Still, a visit to the ruins of ancient Minoa, at the top of Mountoulia hill, very close to Katapola is quite interesting. But Chora remains the most beautiful part of the island.

Chora made me feel the same excitement and the following years, exactly like the first time. Amorgos and I had grown up and in a way, had some kind of comfort in our lives. This has certainly brought some changes. You know how these things are. Aegiali was not the same anymore; not even the villages around –where we were going all of the time back then. It could not stay the same with all these trendy bars which had opened to satisfy the Hunters of the Lost Vibes. At the same time, some exceptional hotels have been built on the mountain. Hotels full of luxury, indeed. Of the kind that you can find in every decent island of the world. Of the kind that you can find everywhere. And when you stay in one of these hotels, it just doesn't matter where you are exactly. And you are just an ordinary tourist, like every other one –nothing bad to this.

The hipsters are still in the sand; most likely not the same ones, maybe their children. I would like to go to Amorgos with my own daughter. I don't know what it will have been left from the 80's. But we will definitely go to Chora. Some things –fortunately- never change.

Anafi

The last summer of the twentieth century I founded a publishing house which I called "Anafi". The first and last book published was a compilation of Indian poetry. Were there any Indians in Athens? Maybe, but they were not enough to make me avoid many financial difficulties and other catastrophes. The following summer I had to work as night watchman in another island, Samos, in order to make it through. Then followed three or four years full of debts, disappointments and not unexpectedly, loneliness. The perfect picture of the catastrophe that was initiated there. From Anafi. Do I love less this island for this reason? Not at all. It keeps always a special place in my heart and nothing, absolutely nothing can change that. According to the legend, Anafi was suddenly emerged in the Aegean Sea after the command of god Apollo, in order to help the Argonauts. To me, there is nothing more real than that. The modern Argonauts are still there, wearing just one −not necessarily golden- fleece or not even that.

Anafi was another place of my utopian dreams. A magical island. An ideal island. And it still is but not for the same people anymore. Why's that? Well, because Anafi was the perfect dream of a completely rebel life, practically led by the waves. There, people looked alike, more than any other place. Life there, summer life, although many brave ones were keeping on till winter, was a unique life, the kind of life I wanted to live forever. Imagine what I would say if the sun didn't burn me mercilessly every day, if I had been there with a girlfriend, or if I had lived a great love there. Still, this feeling was more than enough. Air was full of carefreeness in Anafi. Sea was ours in Anafi. There were no categories of people nor tourists there. The Beast did not exist in Anafi. Anafi was a huge company of friends who were feeling good, without even needing to talk to each other. The sole distinction existed in Anafi was among the new ones, who were staying in the first beach, Klisidi, the older ones who were staying in the next one, Katsouni or further down in the beach of Roukounas and the "ancient" ones who were staying in the end, Megalos Potamos (Big River).

There were also the nude ones and the even more nude ones. There was, and there is still, Chora, if not the most beautiful town in the Aegean, definitely the most imposing and authentic one. There was also the Monastery of Panagia Kalamiotisa, in the end of the route, necessarily by boat or for the stronger ones, on foot. The ascent until there; something like a pilgrimage without any pilgrims. And the view from there; I have never seen the Aegean so transparent, so wide that reminded me of infinity, so provocatively blue. *There, you can see the Aegean Sea like a plate*, they told me once. They were right. The night I spent there was almost a metaphysical experience. And Chora, standing over there high on the rocks, proud, fearless, alone and spread as a warm embrace. I should also mention Drakontospito (Dragon's House), a cave in the north side as well as the road (the only other road) in the west that leads to Prassa and to a few more beaches. However, as far as I am concerned, Anafi is mainly its southern part. Chora together with the rest of the area, from there to the Monastery. For me, at that part of the island, you have just everything.

I will share with you something I heard when I was leaving, because at some point you will leave (why do we always have to leave anyway?). On my way into the ship of return, a girl next to me was saying goodbye to a guy. As he was leaving, he told her this incredible thing that I have thought about many times later on. He told her: someone will come (he said his name, I don't remember it anymore, a common Greek name). *You will meet him*! Can you imagine that? The girl would meet (it was a sure thing) some guy for whom she didn't know anything but his name, a common name. She would meet him because this person would come to Anafi. And in Anafi it's certain that you will meet them all. We are talking about tens, maybe hundreds of people who were arriving every day in the island. Can you think of anything more beautiful? Anything more magical for human relations? I don't know about you, but this still goes with me and I often think of it.

Patmos

Chalki

 *(Greek: Dodekanisa, literally: Twelve Islands)*

Patmos

I remembered Patmos again at the end of 2012, when I read that Forbes magazine chose it as the top among all the idyllic places of the world – an ideal place for someone to live. I was never a reader of the magazine, but I cannot but applaud this choice. I adore Patmos. But I just need to be on the safe side with my other favourites. Writer Paul Adkin, who knows Greece very well, has written that *every Greek island is a goddess and it would be better if one would not pick just one of them, because goddesses are awfully jealous.* So I would simply add a comma after it and continue on with my list of Greek islands. Would I like to live on Patmos? Well why not. The sure thing is that I have been there four or five times and I cannot wait to find myself yet again wrapped in her embrace.

My first time was kind of funny. The ship got there around midnight, maybe even later. I disembarked with my backpack and saw another guy with a backpack who looked friendly. He must have thought the same because he said "hi" in English, to which I also responded "hi" in English. Even one word was enough to understand that our English was not up to scratch and that we were both Greek. "Well," I said to my new friend (I only remember now that his name started with "Th," it might have been Thanos) *"what do we do now?"* He pointed toward the "real" foreign tourists who were already moving in a particular direction without any hesitation.

"So, let's follow them. Foreigners always know where to go to."
And that is how two Greeks followed some foreigners to find a place to stay in the middle f the night in a Greek island. And of course, the tourists knew where to go. After we walked along following them for a while, we arrived at

the campsite at Meloi and stayed there, not only for the night, but for the rest of our days on Patmos. You may have already guessed that I am sensitive enough (even in a silly way) when it comes to islands, but my first introduction to Patmos surpasses every precedent. Think about it: I was young, on my first big, lone journey to the islands, and maybe even happy. So I fell in love with everything.

I fell in love with the path that led to the castle, the castle itself, the Aghios Ioannis Theologos Monastery (Monastery of Saint John the Theologian), the Holy Cave of the Apocalypse (Saint John the Evangelist wrote here the Apocalypse in Meloi), the town, the narrow streets, the painter who drew tiny paintings on pebbles with so few colours (they were, however, expensive for me), the hills all around, the water of Patmos, the calm that had been imposed by the law due to the presence of the monastery – no loud music allowed at night – the small villages, the white houses, the desert beaches, the empty beaches, the sand and the rocks of Patmos. And I also fell in love with almost all the women who crossed my path. Actually it didn't happen even to talk with any of them, but that is irrelevant.

I just hated the Italian fans who shrieked their brains out some nights because their country won the World Cup in football, but that is another story I would like to forget. I have always supported – and will always support – Brazil. Well, anyway, that was my first visit in Patmos.

I came to Patmos again, but not on my own. I –even- came with my wife, once I got married.

I went up to the monastery again and again, I went down the stairs again to the cave of the Apocalypse. I tasted the sweet almond pastries again and again in the small pastry shops, inhaled the scent of jasmine on the patios surrounded by bougainvilleas, stayed up late in bars, hung out for hours in the coffee shops and the small tavernas. An experience that stands out in my mind as unique, and almost metaphysical, is the one I had on the shore that was close to the town centre, from which I swam to a tiny island opposite. It was nothing like crossing the English Channel, but it was enough to make a lazy swimmer like me proud. Nevertheless, there was more to it than that. Perhaps it was the crystal clear, aquamarine water, in view of the almost deserted coast of the Livadi tou Pothitou (The Meadow of the Desired one) and the island of Aghios Georgios (Saint George) drenched in salt. I got the feeling that it was one of those days, or hours to be exact, that comes only a few times in your life, and it usually happens when you haven't even planned it. For a while you believe that you have found the meaning of life. Then you lose it again, but the memory remains.

What would I suggest for Patmos today? That's a tough one I think I already mentioned it in my slightly delirious memory of the basics. If you are interested in Monasteries, it is easy to surmise that there are a lot. The Zoodochos Pege Monastery (Life-giving Spring) and the Koinovio tou Evaggelismou (Commune of Annunciation) at Kipi (Gardens) are two options. If we're talking about beaches, the ones you shouldn't miss are Graikos, Kampos (Fields), Bagia, the amazing Diakofti and the (still I hope) exotic Psili Ammos (Fine Sands), accessed by path). The same goes for Agrioleibado (Wild Field) with the island of Aghia Thecla (Saint Thecla) opposite. And there's one more Livadi (Field) – the one of the Kalogiron (Monks) – found in the north. That side may be the most interesting part of the island. But there is so much more. I also would like to note that every summer there are excellent cultural events – such as the Religious Music Festival at the end of August. I hope that it has not been downsized or even cancelled due to the economic crisis.

Since that night in1986, the island has suffered many injuries and wounds. (People build, build, build – and illegally as well. But in Greece the meaning of this word is not the same as everywhere else – in Greece "illegally" usually means that the state has encouraged you in some way.)

The same happened to me. I endured many changes, injuries and wounds.

My love for Patmos has not waned, not in the least. Would I live on Patmos? Of course I would. If I had twelve more lifetimes, I would definitely give one of them to Patmos. Wouldn't it be great to have more lifetimes so that I could really enjoy all of the many islands (and more lifetimes to enjoy the company of certain women; but perhaps I am asking too much). I would most definitely live on Patmos, but not only on Patmos. Every now and then, I would journey to my other favourite islands. That is the only reason to leave an island: to see another one. Well, a small paradise is only a short distance away. It is such a short trip that I cannot resist the temptation and off I go.

Lipsi

I have talked a lot about my favourite islands and about paradises, about places one wants to live in and about islands where you feel that life is greater than it usually seems. But this island has something more and it holds a special place in my heart. It gave me – this small island and another one that is also rather small, Schinoussa – an overwhelming feeling of happiness. When I talk about Schinoussa, love comes to mind. Love not only for the woman I went there with, but also love for a piece of land surrounded by the sea and ultimately, love for life itself.

I loved this island from the first minute I set foot on it. The truth is that I didn't go via Patmos, which is the usual route, but from Samos. It was a beautiful trip, with the necessary tempest which rocked the little catamaran that was destined not to bring me back. It broke down on the return journey. Maybe it wanted to stay in Lipsi forever, it's hard to say. I wanted to do the same, but what we call real life was calling me back and I didn't have the strength to feign a breakdown.

There is always something special about little islands; I think that I have already tried to explain it. Maybe, in the end, you are overtaken by a modest feeling of possession or ownership. The smaller islands win me over more easily. Take Lipsi for instance. A small port, big enough just for the ship to be able to come and go, small houses, some fishing boats, a few small tavernas. (In one of these I tried olives for the first time. Yes, it's true: until I was thirty I refused to try what is the main product of the island where I was born). A feeling of serenity fills your body, a feeling so vivid and true. No one pays any special attention to your arrival. People have learnt to live without you, the tourist I mean. No one will go out of his or her way to welcome you, or even worse, come to the port to screech his or her offer of rooms to let.

The truth is that most Greeks ignore the existence of this island. But it is still another island on the map. There are hundreds of them. No one has even gone out of his way to organize an advertising campaign for Lipsi. There are no products for which it is famous. In my view, a real paradise doesn't need a marketing campaign one way or the other. And it remains there, obscured from view, so that only those with a traveller's heart can discover it.

A port always welcomes you. That is the case here as well. However, it is difficult to tell them apart: the Port, the village of Lipsi, the settlement of Kampos (Field) and the beach of Lientos. All of this is right in front of you, as they are really close to each other. But I didn't stay long in this beautiful port. I soon followed a path to my right and I started exploring. Later, I saw that it goes from Papandria, Katsadia, and if after a while you turn right again at Korakia (Crows), it finally reaches Choclakoura and Xirokampos (Dry Field). From the various churches on the islands, the one that stands out is Panaghia tou Charou (Reaper's Virgin Mary – one of the most impressive names for the Virgin Mary I have ever heard). It is situated in the southern part of the oblong island (16 square kilometers). If you stay even for three days, do not miss the boat excursion to Makronisi or Arkous and Marathi. I would suggest that you don't miss, without having to walk all around the island, Platy Gialos (Wide Beach) in the north. What importance do the names have? Well, none really. Even if you decide to stay just for a day in Lipsi, you will see it all. It is exactly this magic that small islands have. There is always the sea to guide you. It is not easy to talk about the little deserted bays, the little ports that I came across every now and then, the few hills that looked like a children's painting. Now that I think of it, the entire island looked like a children's painting and that is the key to understanding Lipsi. But the thing is you have to go there to see how it looks like.

Why would you feel like that for an island? The question could have been: why do you feel like that for a person you see for the first time? Now, I believe you will understand the answer more easily. It is exactly the same feeling. At the risk of being characterized as useless as a guide (and I am useless – for Lazy tourists), I am not going to go into the logic of talking about every single little bay analytically. If you would like, dear traveller, I will confess something.

Paradise is something you cannot share that easily. It's difficult for me to talk so openly and advertise this beloved island any further. I have already told you enough, and I know that you, dear traveller, need no more.

Kalymnos

Kalymnos

There are various kinds of love. The love for Kalymnos is a warm and affectionate love for this lady who welcomes you to the hospitable island, more for travellers than for locals

That is what I mean: Kalymnos is an island marked by the obligatory immigration of many of its inhabitants during the 20th century, with Australia as a destination. Most of them went to Darwin. But even those who stayed remained foreigners. Why? Because they were sponge divers. Do you know what sort of profession this is? I am sure you would like to know, but without doubt you wouldn't want to have anything to do with it. This special privilege belongs only to the heroic Kalymnians. I do not know exactly how many metres a sponge diver has to dive – using the amazing power of his lungs and body – to loot the fluffy treasures from the depths of the Mediterranean. The truth is that while I was talking to the inhabitants there – to be precise, they were the ones talking to me (and you know that chatting with the locals is not my cup of tea, with the exceptions of Ikaria and Crete to a lesser extent) – I realized that I had never come across so many people with such a sincere desire to talk. So the truth is that, after every conversation with a local (who almost always happened to be a sponge diver), the distance for the longest dive on record got longer and longer. Thirty, forty, fifty metres... I believed every one of them, even if it seemed unbelievable. You should have been there to listen to them, but you will be, right? Tens of metres, all with a single breath, an endless battle with the limitations of the body and sea creatures in the sea bed, an endless struggle to be able to survive this way, collecting sea sponges. The ships would leave in the spring and return after many months. But the most tragic part of the tale is the anguish of the ones who were left behind, when they searchingly looked out at the ship which was returning, and the feeling of anxiety about whether their loved ones were onboard. Not all of them came back. And among those who returned, some had lots of problems; not all were resilient, but all of them still ventured out.

For people of my generation, immigration is an old tale, but, alas, the situation in Greece nowadays brings back these traumatic experiences.

Let's move on from the sponge divers. The island today gives off the feeling of raw adventure, but it has many amazing neoclassical houses from many periods of the 20th century and surely most of them were built with the money the sponges brought to the island. Really, every corner of the town of Kalymnos is worth visiting. It is a big enough town (almost 10,000 inhabitants) and not very picturesque, but few places in Greece have so many beautiful houses. But this is not the only thing worth seeing there. First of all, this island, remember, is part of the Dodecanese cluster, which doesn't mean arid landscapes, few trees and wild winds. There are small fertile valleys, land suitable for cultivation, beaches that are mainly rocky although some are sandy, and a town which is a bit scary as far as its dimensions go, but you rapidly discover that there is more to it than meets the eye. Naturally, among these things we must not forget the seafood. The little shrimps are their specialty, as in Symi. I do not even like the sight of them, but I know many that would kill for a plateful, especially now with the crisis. I'm kidding of course (or so I hope). And that's not all.

The route to the island's interior is, at times, interesting and even impressive, if we exclude the part of the journey from the capital that extends toward the north for a few kilometers, along which the Beast has passed – it could not be otherwise. It begins at the port, which is the capital, (in contrast to the Cyclades with its well-fortified Choras, for the fear of pirates) and passes by Therma (Warm areas) and Blyxadia first. If we compare them, the second is better, but to be honest the beaches are not the highlight of Kalymnos. Going up north, the route passes from Chorio (Village), with the Megalo Kastro (Big Castle), Myrties (Myrtles) and Armeos, the beaches of Arginontas and Skalia (Stairs) up to Emporio. I also remember the small and slightly sad, although I cannot tell why, Bathi, on the east side of the island. The bay is impressive, but for more bays you would need a boat.

Something I mustn't neglect to tell you is that Kalymnos has evolved into a place that is ideal for climbing during the last few years. The steep shores and precipitous boulders, which was once a reason to leave the island, now draw climbers from all over the world. There are 1,700 marked routes and 60 athletic climbing fields. As of 2010, there is a closed climbing field. It is not one of the reasons I would go to an island, but that does not matter. Approximately 5,000 people visit Kalymnos for this purpose and I am sure they know best.

& Telendos

You must have noticed in the title that I added Telendos to Kalymnos. Well, one might say that I just wanted to include one more island in the guide. How many things can one said about tiny Telendos? It's a small island about a quarter kilometer away from Kalymnos, with a couple of tavernas, some humble buildings and the all-important ancient town. Yes, that's how it seems from a distance. But there, in Telendos, I spent one of the best nights of my life. It was because of an amazing little taverna (I will not tell you which; I am not here to advertise, I just hope it's still there) with an amazing guy who owned it and we all felt great. As the night progressed, we felt even better and finally I felt the rare feeling of being one with the others. When you become one, and you are happy to be alive, to laugh, to sing, to dance, people of yesterday and tomorrow, unknown to each other, but people you could truly love, even temporarily, just for one night... in Telendos.

Kos

I will tell it right from the start. You would understand it, anyway. Kos is not in the small list of my favourite islands. I am not saying it is not a beautiful island; I do not say that it is not worth seeing. Nevertheless, without taking a look at the map, I think that it is closer to Rhodes than Patmos and Kalymnos (let's not get started about Lipsi), which are, as you already know closer to my taste, each for a different reason.

I would say that Kos is Rhodes´ younger sister, sharing more or less the same characteristics. Big, elongated, with an Italian flair due to its history, big beaches, big avenues, big palm trees… This is where, due to the big distances – clearly my issue, my interest gets lost. However, naturally there are lots of things to see. I travelled in Kos, right after Patmos, and the contrast, at least in this era, during the mid 80's, was enormous. In Patmos, after nine o' clock an almost devout silence reigned. In Kos, I saw for the first time, young tourists from the North, lying by their bicycle early in the morning, after an apparent drunken last night. I surely saw other things as well. I saw the impressive avenue with the palm trees along the beach, I crossed it may times, for at its end was the very organized camping site where I stayed. I saw the Asclepeion with the infamous plane of Hippocrates, a bit smaller than I expected, nonetheless. I saw many ancient and medieval monuments, I strolled in it beaches. I stayed up late in its bars, I tasted the local dishes.

I was alone, but never felt alone in Kos; I have to give Kos credit for this.

Let's see closer some facts about Kos. Firstly, it is a big island, the second biggest after Rhodes among the Dodecanese, with vivid signs of a history that begins in Ancient Greece (home of Hippocrates, "father" of Medicine), passes through the Roman era (a tour for both eras in the Ancient town of Kos – do not miss the Villa Romana). The influence of Egypt during the Hellenistic era is obvious (see the famous Asclepeion), till the Venetians came along who let it to the Knights Hospitaller (among other monuments, they built the Knights' Castle (or Neratzies Castle (Bitter orange Castle) and the Antimachia Castle), later the Turks and finally the Italians (they built the most recent monuments) before Kos went full circle returning, after the Second World War, to Greece. But Kos was not popular due to its history only. There are lots of beaches, mainly sandy ones, in all the coasts of the island. However, there is also the classic green environment of the Dodecanese. And as one thing leads to another, it has obtained for many years now, hotel complexes and is the best for the (Lazy) tourist. A way to understand the touristic development in Greece is a (short) visit to Kardamaina or Kamari and Tigkaki. I personally would choose Polemi, maybe Kefalos and Lampi, but surely not during the warm months anyway. A good solution is to take the boat to Pserimos and even there, it is best if you make it to Marathounta. I exaggerate, of course. In an island with endless kilometers of (organized) beaches, do I suggest that you take the boat to Pserimos? This is not a logical guide, I truly admit it.

There is also another option with the boat for a smaller island, Platy (Wide). But do not leave Kos without an excursion in the mount Dikaios (Just) – full of forests, gorges, caves and mainly its villages as Lagoudi and from there to Pyli, and especially Asfendiou.

In the ship back though, I saw the best image of the entire trip. She was climbing the ladder of the ship from Kalymnos, her golden brown hair blowing in the breeze, I could make out her green eyes, and I enjoyed the shape of her body and I dreamed. I dreamed about meeting her and living a story with her. After a while, out of the blue, on the ship's deck, she came and talked to me. Doesn't it sound amazing? It was indeed.

We shared the same big deck of the ship and we slept next to each other, each in his own sleeping bag. At dawn, I took her to the train station; she could not wait to get to Patras to get to another ship to Italy and to her boyfriend who was waiting for her.

You can't have it all, can you?

Tilos

The picture in the back cover says almost everything I would like to tell about Tilos. It is taken early in the morning and embodies the calmness, the serenity, the gentle colours, the loneliness and the blur, the time adds to the sweet memory of Tilos of that time. It is the small, precious, lonely Tilos. That should be enough for you. But I should tell something more.

Tilos is a little island cornered between the Dodecanese and the Asia Minor coastline in the map, very far from the mother port of Piraeus, but far even from the nearby Rhodes.

Were she a woman, she would not be as closed and distant as Nisyros, but neither so open nor pleasant as Kos, surely not so extremely pretty and as boastful as Simi. It would be between all these. And that is exactly how it is. In the map. In fact, it is a very special island, as all of them, and has just two basic characteristics with the neighbouring Nisyros. The loneliness and the ghost-villages. Its port is an amazing example of Aegean beauty and the interior, without being the fertile land of the Dodecanese and Rhodes, is definitely more hospitable that the barren landscape of the Cyclades. It has amazing beaches and at least one that was dreamy, before the Beast approached and now it is merely amazing. Tilos has another strange characteristic, something its position and its geology gifted her, something that is not easy to encounter nowadays. It is the place where you can find traces of the dwarf elephant, an animal that lived there, thousands of years ago. When I tried to get there, I was informed that I couldn't for a reason that eludes me. Greeks bureaucracy (or just laziness) always find pretexts to deprive the joy of seeing some of the strangest sights they have to offer.

But I saw the ghost-villages, I wandered for long in its interior and I had time to love it enough for the few days I stayed there. It was a lonely trip like the one to Nisyros, which took place earlier, I write more below. The important thing is that I went there and I share these lines with you so that I convince you to visit it.

106

Of course you will pass from the capital which is called Megalo Chorio (Big Village), with a castle built by the Knights Hospitaller and the Necropolis, but also from the deserted medieval Micro Chorio (Small Village), while there is also a medieval castle in Messaria. Leibadia (Fields) (very close to the port) is a nice village (and a beach) but I fell in love with Eristos like few beaches in my life– maybe the fact that I was alone there with another camper has something to do with this. The fisherman village of Aghios Antonios (Saint Antony) is a good choice, but do not miss, if you do not mind the boat, the beaches of Skafi (in the North), Tholos and Aghios Sergios (Saint Sergius) (in the South side). In the eastern side, there is the beach of Lethra for those who prefer the pebbles. The route of Libadia, Lethra, Mikro Chorio (Little Village), is one I suggest to those of you who enjoy a walk, although the classical route of the island is called Environment Interpretation Route, where you follow the old path for about 3 kilometers to reach the top of the mount of Profitis Ilias (Prophet Elijah).

The inhabitants of Tilos have respected their island and there is an additional reason for this. Tilos is an example, of how, one man, in Greece, (the country where "we" exists only in grammar), can change even for a small time period the luck of a land. Careful now, this is the first and only time I refer to a name in this guide, but it is really worth it. In a country where it constantly rains injustice (many of these in the area of local government), unfairness, indifference, easy (and usually destructive) solutions, there was a man (he passed away, at just 61 years old, in 2012), who said his "no" and chose his tough path. Tassos Aliferis, mayor of the island from 1984 till 2007(!) was known because he was the first, and in fact the sole, representative of the Greek authorities, who allowed homosexual weddings in his area of administration. But what he did for the communication of the island with the rest of the world was far more important. He alone achieved, using the little power he had, from every point of view, to find and schedule a boat that opened the way to and from the forgotten Tilos. This did not last forever, but it was a heroic act, while it lasted. Later, with the help of the economic crisis, the island went back to its loneliness. Now it hosts, as it had in the past, the passing tourists just for a few hours from Rhodes. However, even needing the extra effort, it awaits true travellers.

Nisyros

Every island is unique, but some islands are …more unique than others. Every island has some similarities with the previous ones, but there are some islands that are hard to find. One of these islands is definitely Nisyros. It might as well be the strangest island that I have seen. Stranger than the crazy Ikaria, than the sacred and distant Delos, even than the mysterious Samothraki (Samothrace).

I went alone there, as was the case with Tilos, during a weird phase of my life, and I arrived after a twenty-two-hour journey (which I enjoyed like nothing else, exactly because it was and still is my big record of staying in a ship to the islands). Proud to finally disembark on the island, I stayed there for some days and the words that I interchanged with the people there were maybe less than the days themselves. When you are in such a phase, then everything seems strange. However, you will see that it was not only the phase I was going through. First of all, the volcano. The volcano that is not only found on one spot, but whose presence haunts the entire island. The volcanic stones, the volcanic type of tourism (because many come here mainly for this) and the volcanic effect that changed the life of the island forever. I was talking earlier about my refusal to communicate with people while I stayed in Nisyros. Communicating was not my strong point, for sure; I listened to them a lot, though. I liked to sit and listen to them for hours, talking in this particular dialect –similar to the Cretan one- narrating stories. Stories that sooner or later mentioned the volcano. The eruption which send away those who had been left behind to struggle with poverty, driving them mainly to Australia and the USA. Stories about the houses that were abandoned forever deserted. Stories about the table that was left laid, as it was forsaken, waiting for the family that left running and never came back. Stories.

The most amazing story, however, comes straight from the ancient Greek mythology and it explains the creation of the island. It is said that it all begun from a war between Gods and Titans. The Titan Polybiotis caused Poseidon's rage (we know from the Odyssey how touchy the sea God was), so he cut off a part of Kos using his trident and threw it towards the poor Titan. This part was Nisyros. So Polybiotis stayed forever buried under it. The volcano´s eruptions are nothing but the moans of the unhappy Titan.

When I talked before about the volcano haunting the island, I really meant it. No island has so many ghost-villages. None has so many imposing deserted buildings which are not for inhabiting anymore or structures that were completed and never functioned or never finished and just their skeleton remains.

And despite of this fact (or because of this), I loved Nisyros a lot. I liked the quiet seafront in Mandraki (when the boats from Rhodes and Kos stop), of course the volcano, which unlike the one in Santorini (much walking about nothing) is still alive, even the inhospitable black, grey or white pebbles on most of its beaches. Nisyros, with its deserted villages and the scattered, huge buildings, abandoned for a long time, definitely created awe but it is not scary. Not anymore. It looks as it is in the service of a touristic development which has not got the power to alter the wild character of the island, as it has happened elsewhere. For the Lazy Tourist it could just be a sight of Rhodes. The boats that connect the two islands come and go till the afternoon. But how can one see Nisyros in a couple of hours with a stroll down Mandraki and a hasty visit to the volcano?

Nisyros is worth more of one´s time. But I would not say that its strong point is the beaches. The port, Mandraki, which has the most inhabitants, has one beach named Chochlakous. It is worth seeing, although I am not personally a fan of bays with big pebbles. However, Mandraki, apart from the fact that it is a picturesque fishermen village, has the old walls of the ancient Paliokastro (Old Castle) nearby, the Monastery of Panaghias Spilianis (Virgin Mary of the Cave), built in a cave inside a Venetian fortress, but Thermal baths as well. Leaving this spot, this is where the adventure begins, as there are just three villages, Paloi (here is the Lefki (White) beach, the only one with white pebbles in the island), Emporios and Nikia and many "ghost" villages – nothing scary, a bit sad maybe, desert islands. There is also, scarce, communication with the nearby island of Giali (Glass), which has really striking beaches. It is an excellent one-day excursion. A really magical beach is Pachia Ammos (Fat sand), it is big, with a strange dark sand and usually reachable (via a path) just for real travellers.

Leaving Nisyros, and after having bought a T-shirt, something I rarely do in islands, depicting a huge map of the island in the middle (still have this t-shirt) , I felt really funny, then a strange thought popped to my mind. That was when I thought: "I am Nisyros". The idea of a lonely and weird guy is always charming. But as it is said: careful for what you wish for. Some lonely years in my life followed, and believe me; they were not exciting at all. But Nisyros was not to blame.

.

Rhodes (also: Rodhos)

The truth is that with big islands I lose my orientation and my style. Both in travelling and in writing style. Rhodes is a good example of this. More opportunities for travelling, lots of sights, huge beaches, huge distances and a big city in the middle, which surrounds an old town, which you cannot ignore nor love. No way. Let's take the things from the beginning. Rhodes is one of the sides of the triangle of the big islands, (Crete, Corfu, Rhodes) which welcome more than half of the tourists in Greece, every summer. They are the small tourist industries of Greece –in actual fact, the last ones left. There, tourism is not a romantic story. It is a way of making ends meet-for the permanent residents. Especially Rhodes has maybe the oldest history of organized tourism in Greece. Obviously, the history, both the old Venetian conquest and the recent one (it was integrated in the Greek state, just after the Second World War) has played a part to this. As in every big picture, Rhodes hides big contrasts inside. The tourist development goes hand in hand with the marks of the Beast; these are not just marks, they are deep scars, but at the same time, being a very big island, it has a series of antidotes that make up to the traveller. No small island can offer you the valley with the butterflies, the beaches of many kilometers, the super luxurious hotel complexes. In addition, the extremely organised and of course very interesting old Medieval town (full of little shops, sometimes cute and at other times boarding kitsch), the easy access with modern ships from Piraeus, Crete, even Thessaloniki and airplanes from all over the globe. Furthermore, Rhodes is the necessary stepping stone in order to visit the small islands of the Dodecanese complex, or the access to them really needs the persistence of a stubborn traveller (and twenty hours, in average, in a ship that always runs late-and that is the easy side during the summer). As with Corfu and Crete, (maybe it is no coincidence that there is no story, funny of melancholic whatsoever here for me, just family trips) I choose ten things (apart for the ones I already mentioned) which I believe are necessary to note for you to see here:

The Lighthouse of Aghios Nikolaos (Saint Nicholas) in the side of the port with the same name, with the famous (although less impressive from up close) Deers and the Windmills from the other side, one of them functions as a Folkloric Museum. With the necessary visit to the Archaeological and the Byzantine Museum, I also suggest the following: the Modern Art Museum in the medieval town, where you can see works of the most important Greek painters, sculptors, and engravers of the 20th century. The hill of Aghios Stefanos (Saint Stephan) with its archaeological site, the stadium of the Hellenistic period and the view to the Old Town is an excellent idea. The Süleymaniye Mosque, in the Old Town is one of the most important sights of the Othman occupation era and a stroll in the Jewish neighborhood will complete the puzzle of the historical information of the town. It goes without saying that you will have passed by the Palace of the Grand Master of the Knights of Rhodes. A building of the 14th century which was destroyed during the 19th century, but was rebuilt right after by the Italians and contains beautiful mosaics (Hellenistic and Roman) the ones depicting the Nine Muses and the Lion Hunting are famous. In the ground floors, two big expositions are presented, with the subject of Rhodes from the Neolithic Period till the Roman Period (the first) and from the 4th century onwards till the occupation by the Turks, the second. All the history of the island is found in these two rooms. Leaving now Rhodes, it is necessary to visit Lindos and see its Acropolis and its archaeological site. Equally important is the ancient town of Kameiros, as well as the Archangel´s Castle, a creation of the Knights Hospitaller, in the area that shares the same name. Given that you will see Faliraki and the bay of Afantos (but you will look for something that is more fitting to you), I would suggest the (interminable) beach of Tsamkika in the east and (at the same side) Stegna (Dry) and Charaki. In Lindos there is also the vast beach of Kalathos (4 kilometres long) and the smaller beach full of pine trees which is called Pefki (Pine tree) for this reason. There is also the Aghios Pavlos (Saint Paul) beach, which is among the 10 best beaches in Europe, according to a voting in the tripadvisor website–I would vote for another, but that does not matter. In the South side, you must swim in Aghios Pavlos and Fourni, but you can also take an excursion with a boat to Prasonisi. If you want to get to know traditional villages, there is the area of mountain Attaburos (an excellent idea is to climb there, it will take some hours, but it is worth the effort) with village Empona and the magical scenery of Epta Pighes (Seven Fountains) in the eastern side of the island. In the southern west side, the most impressive village is Monolithos (Monolith), which has its own Castle of the Knights, another important sight that you should see. These are enough.

Something else: from the airport area in Ialisos (Ixia), to the town, there are lots of kilometres of sea side, full of organised, touristy beaches. Leave them to the Lazy Tourist. Fortunately, Rhodes has space for everyone.

Symi

Symi (also transliterated Syme or Simi)
This is certainly a spoilt child. I do not start in the best way and surely I am not putting you in the right mood. Maybe you have already heard enough about picturesque Symi, about the beautiful port, the colourful houses, the traditional way of life and you really want to see her, you are a traveller, a good fellow and you are looking for something special for your vacations. And now I am ruining it a bit for you. Look, here what's going on. None of these beautiful things are a lie. They are there. With a bit of a good will, you will find everything in Symi. Along with the little shrimps of Symi (which can be found anyway in Kalymnos as well as elsewhere). But, shrimps apart, all these have some increasing tendencies in the last years. This happens, when many people discover a paradise. More people, less of a paradise, that is the way the world goes.

So, the small houses are colourful as always, but they are lots more, as well as their prices to let or for sale. In addition, the port is very busy during the summer months. The boats that go there are more, the same goes for the people who have multiplied, the shops are more and they are not as picturesque or original at least. The beaches haven't grown. They stayed the same. They just seem smaller, because more tourists visit. The truth is that I was not impressed. Apart from these facts, one should take into account the fact that the transportation issues have not gotten any better (possibly all the contrary), the problems of transportation to Piraeus and to the islands, the problems in the field of medical aid (mainly for the locals) while the cultural festival has been facing issues due to the financial crisis.

I didn't have a bad time in Symi. Not at all. I saw a nice island that failed to meet the descriptions. The friend that was with me and had come here, in Symi in the springtime, constantly complained that it was a different island –but it might have been me, in these cases it is more convenient to blame it on the island than to your partner. And here are some things that I can recommend in order for you to have some great vacations, better than the ones of the lazy tourist for sure.

We left behind us the port and we took the bus to Pedi. It is a short but adventurous route which passes by Ano Symi and this is what is more worthwhile, after all. Nimporio (by foot or by boat) in the Northern side, close enough to Symi, is a better choice for swimming. The west side has the beach of Aghios Emilianos and in the east side, there is the beach of Aghios Georgios Disalonas (Saint George Disalonas). Marathounta and Panormitis, two bays in the South are definitely worth an excursion, but even better (with a more difficult access, though) in the same area, Lapidia. It surely worth a visit, going back to Symi, the Archaeological and Folkloric museum. The visit during spring (or autumn) is still a good advice and it does not apply just to Symi. But I know that that is not always easy. In Symi a beautiful movie was shot called "Pachali´s island" (with the amazing Ben Kingsley, directed by James Dearden), which offers an idyllic image from the past. These pictures exist just in the movies of course, but modern Symi (the movie is relatively recent, after all) has many beautiful pictures to offer you. Just do not always believe what you are told.

Chalki

Contrary to many islands that advertise what they have lost in years, the less known and advertised Chalki has all the advantages of an authentic, picturesque, traditional island. I am not sure that its inhabitants appreciate this. Some would rather have less authenticity and more tourists and I do not blame them at all. Times are hard and the neighbouring Symi, seems that it has done all right.

I don´t know if one can evaluate the simple joy of stepping out from the usually small boat coming from Rhodes (since the big boats are in this case a melancholic story of underrating the "smalls") and to be found straight up in the little charming coffee shop under the shadow of the pergola where the locals continue talking about the sea (or politics or sport bets), paying no attention to the visitors. Do not take it personally, traveller. There are islands which have their very own life as Chalki, rich or in the threshold of survival (exactly like Chalki) and they will not make the effort to come and advertise their dow in hotels, pensions or anything else. Chalki needs no touts. If you are there even for a short visit, it means that you have ignored the easy solutions of the lazy tourist and you are looking for something better. You will probably find it, but there is a bit of extra effort involved. You cannot have the cake and eat it too. You will not have here the fantastic offers that make every place in the world look like another similar one. You have not made it till Chalki to meet the joy of an exclusive hotel. You did not spend so much time in the sea to experience organized tourism. You could have done it somewhere else- even in your own country.

Here the sun, the sea, the colours, are a privilege which is for everyone, after all. So for you as well. You have enough places to see in order to add them in your album of memories. Chalki is not big. You can see it all. Let´s start the tour.

Imporios (a name that you constantly run into with many alternatives in the islands) is also the port, the capital and the only big settling of the island. maybe you will stay here (and you will certainly see the impressive Bell tower, the

Castle and the Religious Museum featuring the nice pebble mosaics-as long as you will find it open), but for everything else you will need to walk – at least that is what I suggest. You can stroll a bit to get to Chorio (Village, the old capital of the island). From there, you can choose to climb up the mountain of Ai Nofri or even further towards the Ai Giorgi tou Riakiou (Saint George of the Stream). You can however, walk towards the beaches. Either Giali (Glass) turning towards the South or Areta towards the North –but in this case you must have lots of experience when it comes to hiking. It is no easy feat. The same goes for climbing to the most important sight of the island, the Monastery of Aghiou Ioanni tou Alakra (Saint John of Alakra), 7.5 kilometres from the port. Simpler options include the beaches of Ftenagia and Pontamos, for which you need to walk for just 15 minutes. Now, for Trahi (Rough), Aghia Thecla (Saint Thecla) and the Alimia island, the solution is the boat that leaves from the port. Naturally, there are more. But no one can see everything –certainly not me. That is why I hope I can see the picturesque, authentic and beloved Chalki again.

Ikaria

Fournoi

ISLANDS OF THE EAST AEGEAN SEA

Ikaria

Is it true that if you have lived more time in an island it gets easier to talk about it? I don´t think so. I had a hard time putting in writing the text about Ikaria. Writing about the Greek islands without Ikaria, would be like writing about the history of jazz without referring to Thelonious Monk. So, I finally decided it, one autumn afternoon. And still, with the exception of Crete, Ikaria and Samos are the only islands where I have lived for a long time. Once more I had left my job, I do not remember anymore which of the one hundred different ones I have left in my life, (I have left more, but simply after one hundred I stopped counting) and the idea of spending the winter in Ikaria, after having spent the summer there, seemed amazing. The scenery was very special since I stayed for a while in the thermal town of Therma (Warm Waters), where only hungry cats reside during the winter.

Ikaria, has the reputation of a crazy island, where the inhabitants sleep during the morning, wake up in the afternoon, have fun at night and only think about work when they have really nothing else to do. Furthermore, it has the reputation that almost all of its inhabitants are artists, or at least have a bohemian flair and are extremely friendly with you, up to the point that you feel part of the game from the moment you set foot on it. As with every other myth, there is a part of truth inside −and a big one as well- and a part of exaggeration. During the two last decades, the Beast passed from Ikaria as well. It did not achieve many things, but surely things are not as they were until the 90´s. The myth of the hospitable Ikarian, who will welcome you and open his house for you, became more of a myth during that period. The freaky paradise of the area of Na became a place of totally controlled touristic development. The beaches of Ikaria acquired the side effects of what is known as development in Greece −but only by the people whose wallets become full because of it support this so called development. But that is the way the world goes, as my favourite Kurt Vonnegut would say.

But things are not as bad. The godly madness for which the island is famous for has not abandoned it completely. Now that we mention it, an island whose story begins with Icarus, continues with Ancient Greeks, Romans, Venetians, then gets to a weird phase where it reached a short-lived independence of its own can be nothing but ordinary. Then Greece took Ikaria in its arms to make it soon an exile land for the communists. Not even the terrible fires of 1993 (no one found the cause, indeed anything foul that happens in Greece has a cause, but on the other hand anything beautiful begins without a certain plan, remember this). The absolutely pretentious craziness of the tourists from Athens whose summer raids (always seeking the "authenticity") is not any less, but it did risk rendering the island fake, shallow and pointless. They surely have not managed to do so. But the village, Christos stis Raches (Christ in the Ridges), is not exactly the same, although everything starts late there.

If you want the real Ikaria, listen to my advice and get to know it during an off season period –I know you are sick of reading this. This is the case of course for many other islands, maybe for all of them, but Ikaria, with its weathered authenticity during the last years, gets it back with the first autumn showers and it stays there almost till the summer. Even thus, during the summer months, it is still an amazing place. I know what I am talking about. I know what I am talking about. And it is worth touring it all, and not just a part of it, even if this is not easy without a car. Just do not go during the winter in the sad and desert little village of Therma. For me, now, there is not a more melancholic place in the entire world.

So, let's take a look at Ikaria. Firstly let's disembark at the port, Evdilos, let's stay there even for a short while and then just start towards the west, the beaches, Gialiskari, Mesachti (Mid Shore), Armenistis (Sailor), (all amazing even when packed with tourists) and let's get to Na, but let's not stay there. The most demanding travellers must reach Psaropounta (the point of the fish). In between there is no way you will not go up the legendary village of Christos Raches. A big part of the island myth begins from the lifestyle of the inhabitants here. Let´s go back again to the port and let´s get ready for a long journey till Aghios Kirikos (Saint Kirikos). It is nothing but a relatively quiet village, in between touristic "development" and authenticity. This is where another series of beaches begin, not so impressive, that is true, as the ones at the side of Evdilos. The scenery, at any rate, is different, it looks as if you have met two different islands. Between these two micro-worlds, the area around cape Drakanos, with the Castle bearing the same name, is where the huge stones created the legend of the Dragons. The most impressive is, according to my opinion, the castle of Ikaria, in the centre of the elongated island, on the top of the mountain, in the area of Kosikia. It is another location where you think you are found in a very special place. Ikaria, if you give it time and do not opt for the easy touristic choices, will be one of the most magical trips of your life. I fully believe it. It was the case for me, anyway.

Later, way later, I returned to look for the traces. It was pointless, I could not find them here, not there, not anywhere, I was just seeking for a bit of consolation in Ikaria –and I found it. It was winter again and I remember that I talked with more people than in the time till then, in my entire previous life- remember it is not my strong point to start the chit chat in the islands. I met Odysseus (Ulysses) the dockworker, a cold dawn in Armenistis (an amazing guy-living history of the island), a cheerful farmer here, a tired woman there, and a desperate love-struck one in the rain, all of these that now seem distant and completely cinematographic. I was at stake to end my travels once and for all, as well as every trip, when I got lost in the fog, while driving with the motorcycle in the mountains. I do not know what the whole point of all of these was, but I have not returned to Ikaria since then. But naturally, as with all the big loves, I have not stopped thinking about her.

Fourni

Fourni might be the ideal island for this part of the Aegean, in a micro scale always. In a way it does not present the craziness of Ikaria, nor the comforts -and the green, to be honest, of Samos, but it has something that its two neighbours come short of. Authenticity. Stay long enough to watch at least a fair in Fourni and you will understand what I mean. Nothing that the tourist guides can advertise in big, capital letters, but more from the islands of Greece of the decade of the 60's. Time has made a small stop in Fourni. Maybe it has not stopped completely, but it seems to move slower. And no one seems unhappy, both inhabitants and visitors. I did not stay for long, so I cannot give you a tour, but I stayed long enough to suggest that, if you find yourselves in Ikaria –during the summer there are daily boats- you go and visit Fourni without a second thought.

Samos

The attentive reader might remember that I worked here during a summer as a night watchman (see the adventures in Anafi). And this is just one of the phases I have passed here. I honestly do not even remember how many times I have been to Samos. I have lived for an entire year here with a woman and a cat. Then the woman drifted away from my life, as well as Samos. I was left with the cat. And the memories. Yes, I definitely know Samos well enough, maybe more than I should.

I have loved Bathi (Deep), with its amazing big bay, the largest one, if my memory serves me right, of a Greek island, the touristic but strangely enough serene town, one of the biggest ones in the Aegean, with beautiful old houses, even if some of them are deserted, with the ugly new buildings, constructed here and there, as almost everywhere, with the pretty slope from which your sight reaches to the infinite horizon, with its busy beach full of coffee shops and restaurants that despite of their frequency, do not ruin your mood. I have loved Kokkari – not so much during the summer months, I have even loved Pythagorio, which unfortunately has not maintained any geometrical harmony, but is full of scratches from the kitsch side of the Beast, I have liked Karlovasi, the part of the island with the most "island" feel. I have felt awe in Heraion (the ancient temple of Hera, queen of the Greek gods) with its vast archaeological site and of course I have loved the mountain villages, once inside of a dense forest, now wounded by the fires that marked the life of the island, but still stunning as always. I like this big island, and I wish it would be even prettier, it could be, but I have accepted it as it is and I advise you to do the same.

I have walked more here, than anywhere else, I have walked from Bathi to Pythagorio and from Pythagorio to Heraio (sure, not on the same day), I have walked from the mountains to Heraio (but only because my motorcycle suddenly stopped, to be completely honest) and of course, due to my job, I have walked a lot in the area around Pythagorio at night. One of my duties was to check if everything was all right in various closed archaeological sites (alas, really closed, with lots of precious relics resting there, hidden by the visitors, tucked into dark storehouses, but what can one say about the stupidity of the Greek state). What I can also definitely suggest is to get to the Eupalinian trench. It is an ancient tunnel (to be precise, two parallel tunnels) in the mountain area near Pythagorio, an amazing feat for the standards of the 6th century. No way would I consider the current Greek state to be capable of the construction of something like that. I also found interesting the Folklore Museum which is near there, near the village Pagondas. Of course, after having visited the Archaeological Museum in Bathi and some of the archaeological sites in Pythagorio (there are many of them) and of course Heraion. It goes without saying that you should take a tour of the mountain Karbouni (you cannot say that you have seen in Samos unless you do this) and its villages, I just hope it will never suffer any fires again. In addition, I would like to introduce you some beaches as the ones in the in the area of Marathokampos, in the south west side of the island: Aspres (White ones), Psili Ammos (Thin Sand) and Limnionas. It is a big journey to get there, but it is worth it. And if you took such a big journey till there, maybe you will have no problem in continuing a bit more - and in a tougher path- to get to the beach of Aghios Ioannis tou Eleimona (Saint John the Charitarian). From the north side, apart from Kokkari, some prefer Avlakia (Streams) and others Lemonakia (Little Lemons), but you will pass by Karlovasi and get to Potamos (River) as well as the beaches of Megalo and Mikro Seitani. But for some reason the image of one of the small beaches in the east side, I do not even remember if it was Mikri Lakka or Mourtia, is etched in my memory. What difference does it make? Samos is a really beautiful island. Talking about all these, the desire to see it again rises anew. And as I told you, in the beginning, a love with an island bears this privilege. You can come back whenever you wish to.

Chios

This is an island which has been closely related to the painful side of the Greek history. If you haven´t heard about the painting "The slaughter of Chios" (by Eugene Delacroix), I can tell you that it symbolizes the suffering of the Greeks during the independence war against the Turks. If the opponent was the Ottoman Empire then, nowadays the opponent is mainly other Greeks. Because if you did not know it, there are at least two basic categories of Greeks. Those who love their land, believe in things, respect the others and those who take advantage of the first category. The latter, as bad girls, go everywhere and make the first´s life hard. One cannot say who set the fire and destroyed the natural beauty of this island (as well) during the summer of 2012 and possibly the culprits won´t be found. In this country, the following rule is valid: the bigger the crime, more chances are of the culprit to be left unpunished. The result: one country full of wounds. And there are no Turks nowadays to put the blame on them.

The natural beauty of the island, however, as it often happens in Greece, is made by a very resistant material and it survives. Deeply wounded, but it survives. Visiting Chios this or another summer is worth the trouble. No fire can extinguish its beauty. It has a nice town (wildly developed and spread widely across the beach and towards the inside), it has even nicer, lovely, picturesque villages, known as the Mastic villages, even if the mastic trees (the symbol of the island in a way) are less, there are still enough and there are also other villages. First of all, Mesta, Pyrgi (Tower) (a medieval village per excellence) and Olympoi are the first stops. It goes without saying that you should rent a transportation medium if you really want to see them. You can never see such an island with a bus – the average distance from the capital is 20 to 25 kilometres and the route is too nice for you to enjoy via the bus. In the North side, Vrontados where the site with the (supposed and slightly left) tomb of Homer is found as well as Kardamyla are nice small towns, whilst in the North west there is the possibility for a more interesting excursion to

Volissos and the deserted village of Anavatos (Unreachable) –maybe the most impressive of the island. Kalamoti and Armolia are some of the most beautiful mastic villages that cannot be ignored. There are more beaches, some of them excellent, the most well known one is Mavra Bolia (Black Stones), but I would also recommend that you visit the bay of Emporios in the South, where there is the typically black (due to volcanic rocks) beach of Mavros Gialos (Black Bay) and the beach of Agia Markela in the West. For the rest, which is a lot, there is always the possibility to get to know them with the boat which makes the tour of the island.

There is also the choice of an easy excursion to Turkey, to Tsesme (a distance of a bit more than half an hour) and from there (with an organized excursion) visit Izmir (Smyrna) and Ephesus. Let's not mention the excursions in nearby islands of Oinousses and Psara that are also definitely worth the trouble.

If you go to Chios with the plane, I hope you won't come across what happened there during the last year with a plane that could not land in Chios because the employee was late getting up that morning. That is why I always suggest you go for the ship. All right, I am kidding, but the incident is real.

Let's go back to the town which can provide hospitality and can offer you whatever you want as far as prices are concerned. It will also present you with the stroll to the Venetian castle and visits to the Archaeological and the Byzantine museum, as well as the library of Adamantios Korais. Apart from these, the solution might be to rent a car, unless you want to live the experience of a typical Greek town – unquestionably not so exciting. When I went there with my girlfriend (our relationship ended in the ship back, but Chios is not to blame for this) I decided to stay there and I cannot say that I enjoyed it.

Chios persists and awaits its travellers with its peaceful locations. And it will always persist, I imagine, (after passing the hard time in the summer of 2012) against the Greeks of the category we mentioned before that are fond of catastrophes. There will come the day when they will disappear. I am not optimistic about the fact that this will occur while I am still travelling, but some day, it will surely occur.

Lesvos (also referred to as Mytilini)

This is also a big island; this one also receives many visitors every summer. But is does not belong to the triangle of the big ones of the touristic industry (Crete-Rhodes-Corfu) and this should be seen with a positive eye. If the question that starts with every journey to an island is how authentic it has remained, then the news are good for Lesvos. Its size allows many options and the relatively less significant tourist development gives us more of these choices in an authentic packaging. I am under the impression that this is the island that offers you the most surprises during your stay. We are talking about the Kastro, the churches and the monasteries, the wetlands, the museum of Theofilos, the Museum of the Olive tree and the Folklore Museum. I would like to mention Theofilos, the innocent as far as art and character self taught painter, who often gave his paintings away just for a meal (at the end if the 19th century) while today these pieces of art are of the most representative specimens of the Greek folk civilization. The Museum which is dedicated to the painter is found in his homeland, Varia, near the capital. Let's continue, without forgetting to mention that Lesvos is always a home for poets, starting with Sappho, Alcaeus and getting to Elytis, the Nobel Prize winner.

In the island reins a huge town, for the standards of a town in a Greek island, whereas it is the port that welcomes you first. There is the Kastro, the Archaeological, the Byzantine and the Folklore Museums (among others) and very nice buildings, as well of course many and interesting signs of the large history of the island, but it has also the inevitable bad sides of every Greek town that got bigger (during the previous decades) without any planning or prediction for the future (which is here already), resulting in sometimes bearable and at others unbearable confusion of people and vehicles. But Lesvos is a big island and you will not leave without visiting Molyvos, Plomari, Petra (=Stone) and even more Agiasos and the typical fisherman village Sigri. This is where the amazing forest of fossils can be found.

Near all these areas, there is a beach. My choices: Kagia, Eftalou, Aghios Stefanos and Skala Mistegnon. In the island there are lots of curative fountains. If you are looking for something like that, Lesvos is the place to be.

I cannot leave out Eressos. The first time I travelled in Mytilini, which is another name for Lesvos, I was accompanying a friend (the girlfriend of an acquaintance – later on she became something more, but that is a completely different story) till we met a bigger group of friends, we stayed in Eressos. I cannot say it was the ideal ambience. I still remember the frowny, almost hostile mood of the women there, not on all of the faces for sure, but on a lot. I had the feeling of an invader, obviously by the need they had to feel the space totally owned by them. Who knows, maybe it was my impression (but it was not only mine), maybe things have changed. I have seen the same behaviour in other groups of people, of course (locals, nudists, yacht owners, fishermen and many more) and I always minded the attitude *"you know, this beach here is ours or you know, we were the ones here first"*. For exactly the same reasons, I see red when I see ridiculous Greeks (and inhabitants of the island) trying in any way they can to hinder or render difficult one's visits anywhere, with the sole criterion their opposing(!) to their erotic preferences. I still believe that the islands, their beaches, the sea, everything belongs to everyone, and I always get angry when someone considers them exclusively his. I should let it be.

Next time I preferred to stay in the town and see the rest of the island by making small and big excursions. Let's do not forget about the ouzo. It is said that it is the best in Greece. I do not know, nor will I ever learn (the attentive reader will already remember what happened to me in Naxos). Nevertheless, I surely want to try again the taste of Lesvos.

ISLANDS OF THE NORTH AEGEAN SEA

Thassos

Thassos is a woman famous for her inner charisma. This is how I see her. All right, it isn't easy to fall for her upon the first sight, even if she is not unattractive at all. Anyway, a traveller is someone who looks more than what lies in the surface. So give her a chance, read on and the result might be a trip there –and a true love affair.

This round island is located in the Northern part of the country and can offer many nice beaches and very beautiful forest "oasis". The Beast, under the disguise of fire, made its way from here as well, to this island that has a history starting with the Phoenicians. But let's just not lose time with Phoenicians, Venetians, Egyptians, and Turks; let's just fly to today in order to get to meet Thassos.

We are talking about the island of a thousand different flowers (we are far from the Cyclades as you understand), there are mountains here that you have to get acquainted with, hovering above the usually sandy beaches that crown the island all around. What's more, it has a compact tourist service system, educated by the frequent visits of the inhabitants of Macedonia who, let's be honest, do not have many options when it comes to finding an island, unless they wish to travel a lot. They have Thassos, Samothraki a bit lower and Chalkidiki that yes; truly reminds of an island. Here again, if you don't necessarily want to rent a car, there are small boats in order to discover the beaches. With the view to getting to know the mountain, there is no doubt, only a car or a motorcycle will do the job. During recent years, more and more tourists discover Thassos and there are many reasons for it.

Thassos is an island with lots of ports, but the capital – which is called exactly like that, Limenas (Port, in Greek, but also known as Thassos), is usually the starting point when you arrive here with the ferry boat from the town of Kavala. I mentioned that it may be necessary to have your own vehicle, even though the island has a quite good transportation network, featuring lots of buses. The stay in the town of Thassos will offer you, if you are keen on this, access to many and important archaeological sites (of the ancient Greek, Roman and Hellenistic period), as well as the Archaeological museum. The Acropolis of the Ancient Thassos, the Sanctuary of Dionysus, the temples dedicated to the goddess Athena, Apollo, Poseidon, Pan, the Cyclopean Walls, the Vriokastro, the ancient Theatre and many more compose one of the most impressive archaeological spots of Greece.

Now we will seek the beaches, beginning from Limena and going clockwise: we will meet Makryammos (Long sand), we will continue to Chrisi Ammoudia (Golden Sandy Beach), we will look for something less crowded in Alyki - The Red One. Here we will certainly have a pause. The combination of a beautiful beach with trees that only stop in the seashore and the ruins of the ancient temple, found near there, is unique. We will find again the organized tourist beach in the Southern part of the island, in Paradisos (Paradise) and we will leave it for Psili Ammos (Thin Sand) and for Tripiti (Holey). There continues a series of little ports which have the compound Skala in their name (a classical name for fishermen villages in every island), till we get back to the upper side of the circle by arriving to the beach of Pachi (Fat). Theologos, Kastro, Rachonia, but Mikro and Megalo Kazaviti are the more necessary stops in its interior. A nice idea is to get to Ypsarion, the highest peak in the island. There the view, but mainly the route (which can be combined with a visit to Theologo, Maries, Kazaviti) contains all the magic the island has to offer. I also note that Limenaria have their own Folklore Museum and in Potamia (Riverside) there is the Museum of the ancient sculptor Polygnotou (Vagi) –the entrance is free. Furthermore, the boats for even more desert beaches (and islands) leave all the time during the summer months from Limena, Limenaria and Poto (Drink). These are only some of the reasons for you to love Thassos. We also said that it might not happen at first sight, but it has all the elements for a love that would last for an entire life. If this is your style, Thassos is the ideal island for you.

Samothrace (also: Samothraki)

This is not just a different island, it is a different world. Every one of the islands really constitutes a small world. Nevertheless, this small world has many unique elements. First of all, the access here is done mainly via Alexandroupolis. This means that you should find yourself in the north side of the country and that is a small problem by itself, which can be solved by plane. Unless you want to cross (even if you come to Thessaloniki) in a way the entire Macedonia and the bigger part of Thrace, I would recommend the train, but I do not know for how long you will stay and how much patient you are – the Greek trains are not the fastest in the world.

So you arrive in Alexandroupolis, which is a quite nice town. But you, after a glance or staying just for a night, you take the ferry boat and get to Samothrace. The distance is not huge. Two hours, more or less. There is at least one journey every morning, during the summer months it is frequent, but, just to be on the safe side, check the journeys on the www.saos.gr/ website.- that is not an advertisement, it is simply necessary, if you really want to know when you will get there.

The first thing that you will see from afar is the awe-inspiring mountain Saos or Feggari (Moon). This mountain spreads its roots in the entire relatively small island and plays an important part in its geography as well as to its identity. Here you will find among others, waterfalls, something rare for a Greek island, with the exception of Crete. Furthermore, you will run into wild goats (again as in the case of Crete), but more of them and more free to stroll around. However, the most interesting element of the mountain and the entire Samothrace is the image of the wild nature, of the beauty that has been left almost untouchable from the fleet of the time – the Beast left defeated this place with the tail between its legs.

Samothrace was the island of the Ancient Kavirians. Who were these? They were the priests of one of the most important religious cult centres of the ancient world. Here, is where there was, and apart from the ruins of the temples you can admire the famous sculpture of the Winged Victory of Samothrace, also called the Niki (Victory) of Samothrace. It is one of the three. As about the other two, you will not find it here, you know the story from other islands. The most precious parts of the ancient history have been stolen. You can see one at the Louvre Museum and the other at Kunsthistorisches Museum, in Vienna. Something you cannot definitely see in Louvre is the temples that are here and something that you will not feel there is a strange aura, that no matter how cold blooded you are, you will realize it still lingers today.

Life in Samothrace only for Lazy Tourists maybe stops in the port of Kamariotisa, where the boat will take you. But of course for the travellers there are many more to see. The beaches, for once, are not the centre of the interest. All the same, you will definitely visit Pachia Ammos (Thick Sand), which is exactly what it says, and is the only beach of the island with the privilege of the sand. The first time I went there, in 1986, I went into a lot of trouble (the dirt road looked more than a path), but naturally, things have changed since then. From there you will be found in Karkani, with a bit of walking that I recommend, but only if you are used to hiking in difficult spots. The rest of the beaches are rocky, something usual in northen Aegean Sea, and this is the most Northern point.

Kipoi (Gardens) is the biggest beach of the island, with impressive big black pebbles, but not of my favourite kind. We had camped with my group of friends for some days in Paralia tou Fonia (The Beach of the Killer), where, apart from the beautiful waters, the strong point is the ambience all around, with the river, the trees and the waterfalls. The biggest waterfall is at the south side, in the area of Kremastos (Hanging). On the same side, you will definitely like Giali (Glass), as long as there are not many visitors.

I would not recommend that you stay for a long time in Kamariotisa. Chora is not too far away. Both the way it was built and mainly the way it has been maintained are impressive. It is also interesting to pay a visit to the Folklore

Museum, but even more interesting is the Archaeological Museum of Samothrace in Paleopolis (Old town). It makes sense because this is where the Sanctuary of the Great Gods is, the most well known archaeological site of the island – and one of the most important ones in the entire Greece. There lie the ruins of an entire city, as in the case of Delos. I should not forget to recommend taking a tour of the island with a boat –starting every midday, and that is a good thing, I detest the early morning boats. This trip is an experience worth living. Surely among the other things you will see in this special island are Vathres, the small lakes formed by the streams in some points of the islands. The most well known ones are tou Fonia (the Killer's) and tis Grias (the Old Woman's). It is said that there are almost 100 of these. And as it goes with most of the things you will hear about Samothrace, you 'd better take it seriously!

Skopelos

Alonissos

SPORADES

Skiathos

This is an island that I know very well. Many years ago a travel website asked me to redact a travel guide of Skiathos which included everything. And so I did. Few years after that, in a strange coincidence, the magazine where I was working chose Sporades for me for the summer travel guide of the magazine, It was in 2005. So I know Skiathos quite well. More than I would like. Travelling and working? It can be done, but it is not always pleasant. Especially when it comes to an island with uncountable beaches. Someone had to count them. Ask me not how many, I have forgot, but there are a lot. I just remember never-ending dirt roads which I crossed with my motorcycle and the paths I walked on foot in order to make it there. The most magical visit was when I spent some Christmas in Skiathos. So fitting for the island of Papadiamantis –because for the Greek readers, Skiathos is the island of Papadiamantis. But who is he? He was a great writer, one of the greatest Greek writers, who lived in poverty all his life. The house where he was born is still there, as a museum nowadays.

So, let's begin. Of course you can find a room in the Town of Skiathos, but you will not stay there. The settlement of Kastro, (also,Bourtzi), as well as the House of Papadiamantis are spots that you should visit. The point where I like most is the tiny island by the port. Anyway, how can you stay here in the Town of Skiathos when there are 60 beaches waiting for you? Koukounaries (Pines) is the most known one, and luckily the environment is well protected there, not from getting overcrowded at any case. In the south part, there are Megali Ammos (Big Sand), Achladies (Pear trees), Kanapitsa and (despite its foul name) Vromolimnos (Dirty lake). Under Monastiri, at Kichries, the homonymous beach is one of the best in the island and it can be reached solely on foot. I would also suggest Troulos, Lalaria (which are not as impressive as the locals describe), Mega Gialos (Big Gialos), Megalos Aselinos, Megalos and Mikros Xanemos. The characteristic names belong to small or big bays or beaches. Especially for the Banana beach there are three different ones with this name, one after the other, I would reveal that as you go on and the Banana (the size of the beach) shortens, it gets better. Only the last one is really worth the trouble. Even more, in the same area, after Aghia Eleni, there is a path to Krifi Ammos (Hidden Sand). In all of these, I would add some very beautiful monasteries, as the ones of Evaggelistria but also Panagia tis Kechrias. Definitely, you will not leave without getting to see some of the Caves; the island has many of them, Galazia (Light Blue), Skotini (Dark) and Chalkini (Copper). Surely, you will take the boat. There is only one hesitation in order to give Skiathos the title of the ideal island. And that would be… the other tourists. If you have not noted, for many islands my suggestion is: not to visit during the hot season. This goes here as well; it goes for the islands that "sink" full of tourists during the summer. A winter in an island, no matter which one, is an experience you have to live. For a Greek, even more, Christmas in the island of a writer who has been identified with the legends and the traditions of the Christmas holidays is something unique –for those you can still understand these things.

Skopelos

I have travelled in many islands, this is true. I have seen many a beaches in my life, coasts of any kind, I have fell in love with many sandy shores —it is strange how the sand magnetizes me- and not really with the bays with pebbles. It is hard to choose: which is the island with the best (sandy) beaches. But this is what I believe about Skopelos. I don´t know, but I imagine that the guides do not write something like that —maybe just the ones made especially for Skopelos. Yet I will try to give a logical explanation.

Skopelos gained my preference, when, after having toured the entire island for the travel guides I referred to earlier, I saw so many wonderful beaches exactly as I like them. Calm, relatively simple at first glance, full of enjoyment when you stay there for a while. Usually sandy ones, never full of people, without the typical interventions of the Beast, that here, at least, when I visited the island, had no luck. There are so many of them. Ok, it's true, Skiathos might have more.

They have a great color. I agree that Amorgos has the infinitive -deep- sea blue. They are not crouded. All right, in Schinousa or Iraklia and some secret spots of South Crete you can find many hidden spots without see anybody. Well, the thing is that I chose this island as the perfect beach-land for me, my blue lagoon I guess, or better said a series of unique blue lagoons. And think that I was not even in love then, I had a good friend as a company and our most usual evening habit was watching the World Cup of football. Maybe that is why in this island I had only eyes for the beaches —and football. But there are more things I would like to say about Skopelos.

Firstly, that I consider it a bit unlucky in the family if the Sporades islands. Skiathos, just as a first born in a family (in our case the bigger and most accessible) took all the tourist wave on its shoulders, leaving whatever was left for the rest. Was this something positive? For my criteria, she embraced the Beast as well and this relationship has already left "her" with scars.

Skopelos remained under the shadow of her older "sister", Skiathos. As far as Alonissos and Skyros go, they had their own history, but we will see that later on. Let's travel to Skopelos.

First of all, Chora. It is just as beautiful as the prettiest ones in Cyclades with regards to authenticity, traditional architecture and impressive location, built on a hill over the sea. This is the best welcome you can encounter, at least in the Sporades. Fortunately, it has been declared protected area with its settlements to be maintained intact (as well as the surrounding villages), and one can just hope that this will be truly respected in the future. Chora and Glossa (Tongue) are the two basic towns of the island, though only the first one can be characterized as such. There are plenty of archaeological sites, monasteries and little churches (it is said that there are 350 churches and monasteries to be found in the island) and lots of amazing traditional houses.

The island is actually divided in two parts, the Northern part is the one which has the most authentic natural environment, while the Southern one has been gifted with the most lovely beaches, all of them sandy –it is easy for you to understand why I like this island. Let's take a look at the beaches through a magical route that begins from one point of the island, Chora and it reaches the other side, at Loutraki (Little Bath), which is found in the area of Glossa. The most beautiful beaches that you will come across are:
Stafilos (Grape), Panormo, Milies (Apple trees), Elio, Klima (Vines), Glistres, Chobolo, the little port of Blo and Loutraki (at the end of the route). There is also a boat from Skopelos to Spilia Tripiti (Holey Cave) or the Drakontospilia (Dragoncave) and from Loutraki to Aghios Konstantinos.

In my old notes I discover as my most favourites: Agnontas, Milia (Apple tree) and Mikri Antrina, near Linarakia, Megalo Peuko (Big Pine tree) in the cape Armenopetra and Limonari (in the Southern side, because there is another one in the northern side of the island). What I lived in Skopelos, is a dream coming true, something like a trailer from paradise: I would arrive at a beach, swam, thought to myself that it is the most beautiful in the island, just to change my mind after a while at the next one -the distance between them is never more than 7 kilometres. I cannot tell if it is going to be like that the next time I will go there, I hope that for me –and all of the travellers that this will be the case. Everything is not amazing there, and the everyday life of the people does not recall scenes from the movie "Mamma Mia" which was shot there. During the last winter, the hospital, due to the financial crisis, lacked basic material (as gazes and bandages) for the patients. It is not the best way to conclude a text for such a nice island, but Greece is not at its best and this has sometimes consequences on the tourist as well.

Alonissos

Alonissos is a strange island. Close enough –not to Piraeus anymore, but Aghios Konstantinos, as well as Thessaloniki and Kavala –but not too close. With many beaches, but, for my taste, not the exquisite, special beach, forever engraved in my memory. Not exactly touristic, but under no circumstances an island for loners. With several marks by the Beast (not so deep, though), but with many ways to escape the routine of the Lazy Tourist. With lots of green, but not the amazing forests that have been left in Skiathos. With traditional colour in some points and with a village - Chora which has quite a German (and English) colour due to many inhabitants of these countries who acquired a house there. The Chora of Alonissos was the old capital of the island, it was destroyed in 1965 from an earthquake but was built later again, while the inhabitants had already settled in Patitiri (Wine-Press), the port that welcomes you to the island. Its name originates from the grape crushers that used to be here, from the times when the island produced excellent red wine. Apart from this, it is a classic, tourist village of welcome. It is not necessary to stay there, but at least you can see the Historic and Folklore Museum.

I have to admit that I was disappointed from Alonissos at first, because I did not manage to see the Mediterranean monk seal (Monachus monachus). Alonissos is famous as a shelter for this mammal which lives in the open sea of Sporades and it is protected –as the wild nature can be protected in Greece, that is to say, under difficulties- by an active society and some inhabitants of the island. I did not expect, of course, to watch the seals playing football on the beach that lied before my feet. I did expect, however, to find someone to help me learn more about them and maybe make the excursion with the small boat to take a look at them from afar. I did not make it; there were no routes at the time. So I continued the route of the beaches, I had a guide to redact –remember. I did complete the guide of course, that is why I travelled for kilometers with a battered motorcycle, and that means that there were many beaches to be visited. The nearest ones to Patitiri are

Rousoum Gialos and tou Botsi, but these are the easy solutions. I will mention some other beaches that I consider the best: Spartines, Bythisma (Diving) (near Marpounta), Tzortzi, Leptos Gialos (Thin Bay) and Lalaria, all in small bays going from Patitiri towards the Northern side, from the sole communication artery that crosses the entire island. In most cases, however, you will need to abandon the normal road in order to follow a dirt road or a small path.

There are also Thalassio Parko (Sea Park), Monastiri tis Analipsis (Monastery of in the area of Geraka as well as the little islands Kira Panagia (Lady Virgin Mary), Psathoura, Gioura which has the Spilia tou Kiklopa (The Cyclops's cave), among others, Peristera (Dove), Piperi (Pepper) and many more. All these can be enjoyed with a little help from the small boats that go daily there and back.

The bad thing in this story is that the partner with whom we were redacting the guide together insisted on driving the motorcycle, although he had never done so. He considered it a piece of cake, as the Greeks usually think just about everything. Sometimes they fall roughly. Relatively injured, we continued compiling the guide, and the driving -with me as the driver. And we saw even more beaches. We didn't live any crazy nights, we usually watched the World Cup of football at night, but anyway Alonissos is ideal for serenity and meditation, nice swims, sea varieties and hiking to the mountain areas, as well as visits in archaeological sites. The tours in the interior is a great idea and you don't need any special explorer skills, the highest point is less than 500 metres. In addition, you can make the route from Patitiri to Chora in less than an hour. Alonissos is an island ideal for highways and byways. But be extremely careful if you decide to use a motorcycle for these!

Skyros

This is the special child of the Sporades. It seems as if it has the same mother, the green mother nature of the other three islands, but its father originates from the Cyclades. Even the wind here, metaphorically speaking, is different. There are more realistic differences anyway. Skyros has no access using the service of the rest of the islands, you get here with a ferry boat only from the small town Kimi of Evvia (it will take you two hours from Kimi by boat, but Skyros has an airport as well), while its architecture makes you feel that you are in a Cycladic island. So Skyros had its own life. She is more picturesque; more isolated than her island sisters and has her own special history. It is a strange "Ugly duckling", left in the family of Sporades and it will not give away its secrets easily. As a memory of its name (Skiron in ancient Greek is the ruins of a stone), it will remind you it is a rocky and steep place –nowadays it gives you the exact opposite impression, unless you climb high in the Southern part. I personally stayed in its valley, fell in love with its beaches, but I admit I loved Chora even more –and especially the magical room in the path leading to the sea that hosted a brief love affair which I identified Skyros with. Maybe that is why I hold a special love for this island, known in the rest of Greece for its little horses, the only place in Greece where these little beautiful ponies live. Chora is a place I treasured a lot, it is also singular, built on a hill, you have to walk uphill to get there and it takes some effort (it goes without saying you must be prepared to hike in Skyros), you enjoy the life there, during the summer, because during the winter it is very lonely and you go down again in a beautiful beach. This happens if you already have not rented your vehicle from Linaria, the port.

Skyros is the biggest island in the Sporades and in order to explore it, unless you go everywhere on foot, you must rent a car and be ready to deal with steep, dirt roads, especially if you venture to the Southern side. This big island, has few roads with asphalt. The uniqueness always comes at a price.

It goes without saying that I recommend staying at Chora with the (Byzantine and Venetian) Castle and the picturesque houses and alleys, where apart from the easy access to the beach (not the best, but a beach nonetheless) and the necessary Archaeological Museum (near the square dedicated to the British poet Rupert Brooke, who lived here for a while and died here), there is also the Faltaits Historical and Folklore Museum, of special interest because you will see the furniture of Skyros as well as small items of everyday use of older times and you can form a clear image of life then. Apart from Chora, Skyros is actually divided in two parts, the Northern west one which is the joy of the walker and hiker and the Southeast, suitable only for explorers. We should add here, that for hikers and mountaineers, there are two high mountains, Olympus in the northern part and Kochilas in the South. And there is also an amazing pine tree forest on the way to Atsitsa, and one of the most beautiful beaches, a Neolithic settlement at Trachi (Steep), whereas for the little horses you should go to Palamari at South East. As far as the beaches go, the most close to Chora are Magazia and Molos (Peer). You do not expect me to recommend these. No. On the contrary, I would suggest Gialos (Bay), Aghios Fokas, Kira Panagia (on the way to Atsitsa), Aghios Petros (on the West), Achili, Mealo and Renes to the South (hard to reach), Kareflou (on the way to the airport) and especially for nudists Choma (Ground), extraordinarily close to Chora (via a path though).

Some extra information, which might turn out useless if you arrive during the summer, but I would like to mention the Carnival of Skyros, a celebration of very ancient origin dedicated to God Dionysus. In general, I am not a fan of carnivals, but this is one of the most authentic of the ones organized in Greece. Improvised theatrical representations, ancient satiric rituals come alive again, traditional dances, poems recitations while the same enthusiasm is given to the celebration of Kathara Deutera (Pure Monday) featuring the local, advent specialties due to the period (the Easter Advent begins at that day). All these info is destined for the visitor during February of March. But this is –fortunately today- an island that always awaits you authentic and still beautiful, even during the hot period of the summer. This "even" includes a danger of destruction of the nature in the southern part of the island for a supposedly "green" (aeolic/wind) energy – actually for an increase in the gains of the powerful Monastery of Mount Athos which controls vast part of the island´s lands!

Hydra

Agistri

ARGO-SARONIC ISLANDS

Aegina

Ah, the sweet girl next door (or next port!). It is so nice there. This island is the first choice for the weekend, especially for the Athenians. It is that simple. Ships depart all the time, winter or summer. The sea is almost always friendly. The breeze has the time to touch you for a while, the permanently hungry seagulls from Piraeus have just abandoned the ship and there you have Aegina with the eternal cafes and taverns in the beach waiting for you. I believe that they have always been there, long before the Greek black & white movies of the 60's which were finding there the easiest island background for their shootings. Even before the tourists. Even before the Beast. It is true that it has passed from Aegina. The port definitely is not the same as 50 years ago. But who is? The signs of age are spread all over the face of the island and make it a bit more attractive –at least for my taste. Agia Marina, Souvala, a place where the Greek dream of unauthorized residences blossomed and Perdika would be more beautiful if it had remained what it was in the beginning: a picturesque fishing village. But it doesn't matter. Aegina kept its serene atmosphere, not necessarily in August when the close to the port beaches are full, kept its friendly mood and it is still an island that worth visiting. It has also kept the ancient majesty. The most well-preserved temple of Ancient Greece is here. The Temple of Aphaea. *(Aphaea was a Greek goddess who was worshipped (14th century b.C.) exclusively here at this sanctuary associated with fertility and the agricultural cycle. Later she came to be identified with the goddesses Athena.)*

The Temple has kept something from its mystical character that used to have at those times. Aegina on the other hand kept a lot of the green color. You cannot ask for more from this island with the famous in Greece peanut trees which make the salesmen running up and down trying to sell their goods (which strangely, are not always fresh) to the passengers who have just arrived there. Even the donkeys which drag the carriages are still there. But I should move from the port, let's see what happens in the inner part.

To be honest, I should recommend you to avoid Souvala and Agia Marina, I think even Perdika, in July and August. A good idea would be to visit Paleochora (=Old Town), the old –as you understand from the name- capital of the island which is deserted now but with a special charm. Not far away, you will find the Monastery of Agios Nektarios, a very important one for the religious Greeks. Also, the mountainous village Pachia Rachi (=Thick Side) next to which there is the Greek Care Center of Wild Animals. The picturesque fishing village Portes (=Doors) as well, from where you will go on your excursion to the ancient Sanctuary of Ellanios Zeus. But what I strongly recommend are the Government House, Markello's Venetian Tower and the Archeological Museum in the capital, the Temple of Apollo and of course, the Temple of Aphaea near Agia Marina. Vagia and Aginitissa are two beaches which you can visit without problem, even in the hot summer months. Next, you will find out some things about the neighboring Angistri island.

I must admit that it not possible to count how many time I have been to Aegina. In a few years, I must have been completing (alas) half century of visits there. What consoles me is that I began these journeys in a very early age as well as that both the island and myself keep on good shape. This is one more reason that makes me loving it.

Agistri

Aegina's little brother has the good and bad that come with "progress", still in a lower scale, as well as the forest, the beautiful beaches and less noise. A family destination, an ideal solution for the weekends. From Piraeus, is less than an hour away and from Aegina around 20 minutes. Ferries leave you in Skala (=Stairs) and the dolphins in Megalochori (=Big Village). What I like to the island? The fact that it never comes to mind as first solution, unless you have a special bond with it. But precisely for this reason, is one of the most ideal "easy" destinations, together with Kythnos. Not that close and not that known to be too crowded and not that far away to have larger expectations. As we have already mentioned, just for a few days or the entire summer if someone has the ability of that. Two ports, Skala and Megalochori sufficiently touristic for even easier solutions, two kilometers the one away from the other. But you should better take the road to the south –some effort will not do you any harm- so as to see the forest. Ignore the touristic Skliri (=Tough) and visit Chalkiada but here you need to go also on foot in a path of about half kilometer. In Dragonera, there is a sandy beach, a small and a big one, to be specific and pines next to the sea in Aponisos.

Now, the bad news is that one of the most picturesque beaches of the island, that is Dragonera, supposed to be the paradise of free camping, is just a dump covered in heaps of garbage left behind by silly (wanna be) campers, especially at the end of the summer season. It is really a disgrace to walk there and see this mess. So, don't even think of free camping there.

Poros

Aegina is the ideal place for the weekends. Hydra is the aristocrat of artistic influences, Spetses a painting called "Happy days". What is left for Poros? If you ask a Greek who lives elsewhere, he will just tell you that it is an island in the Argo-Saronic Gulf. And perhaps he will remember of Lemonodasos (=Lemon forest). A bit unfair, don't you think?

It is unfair, as a local would say, because his island has several beaches, many monuments which vary since the Paleolithic era to the 20th century, many neoclassic buildings –one of the most beautiful is Villa Galini (=Serenity) of the end of the 19th century which was connected to the once prospering cultural life of the island – and many green areas. As a matter of fact, it has the biggest portions of green that you can find in this island complex. Of course, there is Lemonodasos with the thousands of lemon trees spread in a land close to the capital of the island. I would say that this capital is just nice. You could call it picturesque if you think that the typical line of cafes/taverns/bars in the beach and the noise that inevitably prevails throughout the entire day, is something picturesque. Naturally, we refer to the summer period. In winter, the same shuffle remains but it is less hectic. We should better search for more interesting things unless you prefer taking a look first to the archeological museum – open till 3pm- and the Metropolitan Church of Agios Georgios with the murals of the significant painter, Constantinos Parthenis (1878-1967).

The Russian Dockyard is in a short distance from the town and what has left from the buildings created almost 200 years ago, is truly interesting. Also within a short distance, on the way to Ancient Trizina, you will find the Magoula dome royal graves since the years of the Mycenaean Civilization (16th – 13thbC century). Ancient Trizina, not the homonymous small modern settlement, is a must-see sight for whoever visits Poros.

Let's talk about the beaches now. Needless to say that I had been visiting Poros a lot when I was a child. It was a typical excursion of the urban families of Athens and Piraeus back in the 60's and 70's and (just like nowadays) together with Aegina was a more friendly and accessible destination than Hydra and Spetses. So, the beach of Poros was an experience for the years of innocence but not anymore. In the exact same way, the beaches you meet near the town remind of the lost in noise and lounge chairs, innocence.

Alyki, close to Lemonodasos could be the best choice but not for my taste. It looks more like a lake and I don't like lakes. The good thing about this kind of places is that you can reach them by boat, just like Galatas (=Milkman), the opposite side of Peloponnesus –Poros and Spetses keep strong bonds with the inland. Still, neither this one nor Gerolimenas fascinate me (pebbles, taverns, yacht owners, nothing from all these is my cup of tea), not even the beaches in Askeli or the Cove of Love, a bay where the Beast has left its mark. Still, it has left many green parts and this is a thing you could generally say about Poros. Vagionia, indeed, is adorable. Certainly, it is not a beach that brings in mind "Lost" but especially during the "other months" is something. Even more because in the seabed of the sea you can find the ruins of an ancient town, fact that attracts here everyone who enjoy search underneath the sea or/and hunt fish. Personally, I do not want hunt anyone or anything in the sea or elsewhere. But it is better than have them around you.

Poros is the friend from the old days. It is delightful to visit him but not to stay for long. You know how it is: you can talk about anything, but at some point you should leave, otherwise you are bored. It would be better both for the island and yourself. But a visit once in a while won't do you any harm.

Hydra

Hydra has the arrogance of an aristocrat. The last years of the crisis cannot change the habits when we refer to an island that even during Ottoman Greece managed to prosper, unlike most of Greek regions. Besides, Hydra and also Spetses, Andros, Syros and Chios (up to a point) were the dominants of sea trade during the 18th and 19th century. In the 20th century this heritage was translated into imposing mansions and in the case of Hydra, into rules –quite unusual for Greek standards. One rule: No cars in our island. Impressive if you consider the mess that prevails in the rest of the country because of the unaccountability of cars and drivers. Another not so obvious rule: wealthy visitors or at least artists are preferred. Hydra is the homeland of several of that kind and certainly owes a part of its modern myth to the poetic years that Leonard Cohen has passed there. But let's stay to the tourists for a while. Hydra has been evolving the issue of "Good (means of course: wealthy) tourism" for many decades. The formation of its ground that makes difficult free camping, has contributed in that matter. Another factor is the distance from Piraeus and the access with flying dolphins (faster and more expensive than the organized ships). The beaches in Hydra are an issue of their own. In spite of my frequent visits there, I cannot say that I have enjoyed the sea. But beaches is not everything. I have passed happy days in Hydra and the last thing I was looking for was a sandy beach full of people and deck chairs. In the northwest side of the island, you can enjoy your swim in the beach of Palamida and a bit lower in the ever more isolated beach of Agios Kyprianos. In the north side I pick out the beach of Molos and Kaoumithi. It goes without saying that for all beaches of the island, the boat is the best option. In Hydra there are many Monasteries and innumerable churches and chapels. If you had to choose, I would recommend the churches of Ypapanti and Ai-Giannis Nisteftis as well as the Monasteries of Agia Efpraxia and Profitis Ilias. Now if you want to combine them with a walking excursion, you should pick the church of the patron saint of the island, Agios

Knstantinos, the Hydrian and you will follow the path up to the Monastery of Profitis Ilias. But there is more. You can literally see the entire island by walking. Yes, it is not enough just to drink your coffee in Kanoni (=Canon) in order to claim that you know Hydra –although this is precisely what most Greeks do. The morphology of the ground and the vehicle prohibition compose a true paradise for those who love trekking.

It is true that I have traveled many times to Hydra the last few years. It is a typical escape for the weekends when you live permanently in Athens where I used to live. Still, it was magical just once. I sometimes wonder if she remembers of it as well, though I don't know if it matters anymore…

Spetses

It is logical that the more of 4.000 years of history have left their indelible mark on this island. Since the days of the Mycenaean civilization until the war for the independence of Greece in the beginning of the 19th century –with intermediate byzantine and west European influences, let alone the corsairs, this island, perhaps more than any other else, keeps guarded its historical memory –especially of the modern times- and goes on with this. Besides, with this memory welcomes you. Its name Isola di Spezzie (=fragrant island) derives from the plenty fragrant plants. The nice ancient name was: Pytioussa which means Pinophyta. The Old Port, the one you see as soon as you arrive to the island from Piraeus, is a place of glorious history, mixed with battles for independence as well as conquests in financial level. It is impossible to come to the island and not learn some things about Laskarina Bouboulina, the Lady who gave her own battle against the Turkish and of course, the prejudice of those times according to which it was unthinkable for a woman to manage her fortune, let alone a revolution. But it did happen. The most beautiful sample of that power is the old mansions that prevail in the area and impose their architecture in a way that you forget of any ugliness that the Beast has tried to leave on the island.

The house, more accurately the mansion of Laskarina became a museum (right next to the central port) and together with the monuments of her history –her life seems like a fairytale but it isn't- you will be taught a typical lesson of Greek history about the revolution years. Another very interesting building is the Goudi Mansion (mid19th century) but the one you cannot miss is Poseidonio which the last few years is finally being restored in order to remind of the old glorious days.

Something you should know is that the cars are forbidden in Spetses. If this is the case, then what are all these quadricycles that you will see in the roads? Like every rule in Greece, there is always an exception which usually serves those who make the rules. Unlike Hydra where rules are rules, here rules are… not so strictly rules. Be sure that if you want to, you will find a way to bend them. Besides, you have come for vacations to Greece.

Traveling to Spetses is undoubtedly an experience. If history is not of your interest, there are many beaches for you to swim, some of them provide the idyllic picture of the trees that reach the sea. Most of them are what we call "organized" but if you choose a boat for your transport you will discover others, more beautiful ones. Naturally, the temptation is to begin from the beaches which are very close to town (Agios Mamas, Agios Nikolaos) and are not a bad choice but during summer months, you know that already, there will be many people around you enjoying them. The crowd becomes smaller as you go further, you know that also, so some walking will be good both for your eyes and traveling instinct. The beach called "Kaiki" (=Boat) is not that far, as a matter of fact they are two beaches of fine sand which some people may like –I don't really do but this is of no importance. If you prefer, like myself, the more lonely experiences, go on (not necessarily on foot anymore) until Ligoneri (=Little water). The name has nothing to do with the beach, water there is plenty. From this point and on (you have already taken at least the bus) there is Zogeria (the one with pines as we mentioned before) and even further the beach of Agia Paraskevi (you come here also by boat) and even lower (we have seen almost the entire island which is not that large anyway) the beach of Kouzounou.

Let's remember now of the name of the island: "fragrant island". Therefore, many fragrant plants and flowers – compared to other islands- forests, a big mountain, many paths, many options for walking in nature. So, Spetses, at first sight, charms you with the history and later, you discover the adventure. My adventure in Spetses was small but you, traveller, you have every opportunity to have a fantastic time there – if you have what it takes as I couldn't say that Spetses is an island made for the poor. But you can never have it all. Or if you do, there is always a price.

Kythera

Kythera

ISLANDS OF THE MYRTOAN SEA

Elafonissos (Deer island)

Once upon a time, there was a wonderful beach. The sand was white; the colour of the sea was between light blue and turquoise, just cedars all around. The beach was located in a small island at the feet of Peloponnese, which, if you think about, also looks like a foot. That small island took its name from the deers. There used to be deers there. Later, when the deers left, the first tourists arrived. This is where the fairy tale ends and the real life for Elafonissos begins. Of course, the guys who discovered it first for their holidays were happy: free camping in the cedar wood, tents on the sand, an amazing beach all for themselves, later on a bar exactly upon the rock and life can be magical. It is very likely that these pioneers of the tourism respected it completely. Well, the thing is that very few Greeks are real campers and respect the environment -this is bad but true. After some years, exactly in the area of where the free camping was, an organized camping was built. It was just a coincidence that then the police started the raids to the free campers. So life took its course and Elafonissos became from something like a paradise to another island that welcomes tourists and wants to live from them.

I went to Elafonissos on the summer of 2000. The camping was there, but there was also the free camping area. Already the campers were more than the small cedar wood could take (which would become smaller every summer). The magic persisted, if you neglect the fact that you had to accept a paradise with many neighbours. It was a nice adventure. At the beginning, I was on my own, then an girlfriend came and we stayed together in the tent, later for some reason I could not handle living together and I went back to Athens. But Elafonissos was a nice adventure, which begun from the way you get there.

You certainly need a car to get to the little port of Neapolis and from there take the little ship (or better put the big boat) to cross. But even when you did arrive across, you ran into a settlement that had nothing to do with your intention. Then you should walk many kilometers to cross the dirt road which would take you to the beach of Simou. I enjoy walking, but it is not the best scenario having to walk kilometer after kilometer in the middle of the night in order to get somewhere –not even knowing where. Nonetheless, this is how adventures are born. A man picked me up with his car and he was kind enough to drop me on the beach. On the way back, things got even more adventurous. The only choise I had was the little van that served as the rubbish collector of the island! It was in its (fortunately) empty carriage, that I was loaded and driven back to the civilization. Anyway, I had a great time in that island. Everyone was then talking about the changes that were to come in the next years and many already preferred to stay in the new, then, legal camping area. It was the end of the Golden Era, so I should be happy to having been able to even see it. The beaches are still there: Simou (the official name is Sarakiniko) and Fragkou (actually it is the continuation of the first) and Lefki (White), on the other side of the bay. As far as the cedar forest goes, I cannot swear it is there. These were the typical beaches of the Southern side for the campers. There were also the beaches of Tigani (Pan), Kalogeras and Kontogoni in the Northern side. Now, I don't really know whats left.

For someone going to Elafonissos for the first time, he may consider it charming. But those who went there during the first years are now looking for new summer paradises.

Kythera

Yes, the truth is that Kythera belong to the Ionian islands. However, according to certain administration services, they belong to the Prefecture of Piraeus. In my opinion, the most important fact is to inform you that Kythera is an island which is found just under Peloponnese, between three Greek seas: Myrtoan, Cretan and Ionian. This is helpful to understand the island a bit more.

Kythera is the island of Aphrodite. It is not the only one, Cyprus also claims this title, in this case the myth, truly impressive, wants her blossoming form the waters of the sea. Cytherian Aphrodite *«κεύθει»* (hides in Ancient Greek), she hides the love till it finds a cause and it bursts. That is why Kythera, according to some guides, provoke erotic feelings, they magnitise and create a dreamy feeling for the lovers which follows them for all their lives. Don't believe what you read in the guides, but as for me, I spent some amazing days with my then loved one there. I remember the idyllic Aghia Pelagia and a small room to let with blue windows, bursting with pink and red bougainvilleas, a loud fair in a village whose name I forget and an amazingly preserved big village, Potamos (river) and a melancholic Venetian ghost village in Mylopotamos (The Mill upon the River). The exact opposite from the touristic capital, Kapsali, which I must admit was not great. A typical lovers quarrel for an irrelevant cause, which I no longer commit to memory, render the hours I passed there even darker.

I still remember the children´s plane with which we got back to Athens. I am not particularly afraid of airplanes, but it would be hard for me to get back in there, even if you paid me. The pilot looked more like a taxi driver and you would easily fall in the temptation to tell him if he would leave you somewhere closer to your house than at the airport. Years later, a real taxi driver who happened to drive me to Piraeus for another journey, told me that the situation of the communication to Kythera, not only did it not better, but, when it comes to ships, it became more scarce and difficult, for the fast ferry line to the island was cancelled. I could not believe what my ears were telling me, but I confirmed it. In Greece you should always be ready for the worst.

Let's take a tour of the island together: I will take you straight away to a beach (to be precise, in three, progressively smaller, as you keep on exploring, beaches) which definitely makes it in my personal top 10 beaches of Greek islands. I refer to Kaladi. A blue green summary of the magic of the islands is found there, a mysterious painting of small bays, caves and scattered multicoloured pebbles. The Beast has arrived there as well, and no one prohibits them from building closer and closer (apart from the economic crisis!), so you'd better hurry. Fortunately, there is still dirt road as you draw near and stone steps for you to climb, so some very classical tourists avoid it.

Most of these will be found hanging around in Kapsali, which has everything that someone who travels in the same place needs, without him realizing it. For he travels in places that have all become the same, for his sake. There is naturally the Archaeological museum, a reason for you to pass from there, but more importantly, there is Chora, exactly over Kapsali, with its Venetian Caste. This Castle faces to three different seas and constitutes the key for you to feel what exactly Kythera are. I will tell you more at the end. Now, stay there, enjoy Kapsali from afar and go back to the journey to the rest of the island, let's say at Ablemonas (Venitian castle, beach, a joy for family vacations) and if you don't feel the satisfaction of the traveller, there is as I mentioned Potamos, in the middle of the island. It is, for those who like them, a traditional big village. Once Greece was full of them. The word *Mylos* is added to take us to the next village, Mylopotamos, here everything is even more beautiful, because the traditional architecture has been maintained and in the horizon in Kato Chora (Lower Chora, a really fitting name), the Venetian settlement is found, which is one of the places that I love – as with every good horror movie- because they scare me a bit. Why is it called Mylos (Mill)? Because if you get a bit lower outside of the village, you will run into waterfalls and (remember Mylos & Potamos, i.e. Mill and River), there were lots of waters and water mills. There are still there, just for us to see. There is also the cave of Aghia Sofia which adds another piece in the mysterious ambience. In order for us to drift for a bit, I cannot but recommend a tour to Diakofti, the

Northern East side of the island, its beach cannot be left without mentioning, it is beautiful (and would have been even more so if one could push even further from the sea everything that was built in its proximity), but I will suggest two other alternative routes, one in the top of Aghios Georgios (Saint George), where it is claimed that a Minoan temple stood there. The other alternative is crossing the Gorge of Tsakonas.

As far as Aphrodite goes, if you insist on finding its traces, there is an ancient temple, in a small height in Mount Palaiokastro (Old Mount), near the beach of Scandia. Of course, there is an Archaeological museum in Kythera. But what is more important to me is searching for the traces of different eras of the island in its every corner, and not in every corner of its museum.

So what is Kythera? It is not one thing, there are a lot of things together. It is a nice mix of what one can experience in various Greek islands, for Kythera is not a Cycladic island, nor an Ionian island (even if they say so), nor Crete. It is no coincidence I place it in a special category along with Elafonissos. Kythera is something special and it bears a taste of all the regions I mentioned before. If you are fond of mixed flavours, you will be there this summer. And I remind you of something. Kythera (Tsirigo, for the sailors and the older ones) is the quest for happiness. Not the happiness itself, its quest. This −sometimes- is even better.

IONIAN ISLANDS

Zakynthos

This is an island that people have called "Florence of Greece". I am not sure that I can see the resemblance but definitely the Venetians and later the Italians have left their mark in Zakynthos. But the same happened with the French (more precisely during French revolution, an aura of which came up to here) as well as the English. Still, it remains an authentic Greek island and perhaps, the most typical Ionian island. As happened with the rest of them, it was marked by the earthquake in 1953 and naturally, despite the destructions, managed to recover.

The town of Zakynthos, you definitely must spend some time here, has a lot of monuments, mansions and neoclassic buildings and villas which at some cases have been converted into well-preserved public buildings. You must see some of the museums such as the Ecclesiastical Museum and the Museum of the poet of the Greek National Anthem, Dionysios Solomos. Also, you have to visit some of the many churches and the Castle of Agios Georgios. Leaving the town behind, there is a bunch of sights, archeological sites, monasteries, caves –especially the Blue Caves in Skinari Cape and the sea cave Dragounara. There is also, but you'd better not try to search for it, the protected turtle caretta-caretta in the area of Laganas – where many prohibitions, valid from May to October, have been imposed because the area constitutes a National Maritime park. Now the issue of prohibitions regarding such topics is a sad story in Greece. Beyond any prohibition, it's not a common sense for the modern Greeks to accept that we must (I am talking as a Greek) preserve in any case a place of special beauty. But let's talk about the beaches. The good news is that Zakynthos has many beaches and the not so good that there are too many tourists during summer months.Laganas, Banana and Navagio (=Shipwreck) are famous. That is why I will recommend some others. However, I note that for Navagio there is a boat but it is a bit expensive –perhaps crisis decreases this also.

I would pick Argasi, Kminia and Sekania in the area of Vasilikos (=Basil). Instead of going to Laganas, I would recommend to walk a bit further to Agios Sostis or take the boat to Marathonisi (=Fennel Island). In the west, there is the isolated, if something like that is possible in summer, Roxa beach and in the east, among many others, Ammoudi, Alikanas, Alykes (=Salt flats), Makris Gyalos (=Long Coast) and Skinari.

Perhaps, another useful geographical information is that the "greenest" part of the island is the one that covers the east side while those who prefer mountains, paths and in general the mountainous adventures, should direct to the west side.

Finally, I shall say that Zakynthos is accessible by plane (the airport is in the area of Laganas) and ferry boat from Kyllini, a small town in Peloponnesus (mostly known for the therapeutic natural spas). In summer there are from three (Saturday & Sunday) to five schedules (for weekdays). The journey from Kyllini lasts about an hour and almost never reminds of the infantile adventure which I am so proud of, the one I describe in the beginning of this guide.

Kefalonia

The most bizarre extraordinary among the Ionian islands is Kefalonia. They say that people who live there are obstinate and stubborn while others just call them crazy. This is true, in a good sense. And there you have a mixture that you will not find in any other place in the Ionian islands or anywhere else. It is a big island of its own tourism wihout reaching the levels of Corfu. It is not as cosmopolitan as Corfu nor as calm as Lefkada or as picturesque as Zakynthos, although especially the villages are almost equally beautiful. But Kefalonia has its own assets and if you are fond of strong characters and strange locations then you are in the ideal island which also has magnificent beaches. If you have watched the movie "Captain Corelli's Mandolin" you have already taken an idea.

So, let's see some significant places around the island. I would definitely recommend the Cyclopean Walls (ruins of the Ancient Town) near Razata village. Without question, the Venetian Castro in Assos as well as the byzantine but with Venetian adds Castle of Agios Georgios (close to Argostoli).

Close to Argostoli you will also find the Katavothres (=Sinkholes) *(gaps in the ground near the sea which permit the water moving)* which are more impressive when you hear stories about them rather than looking at them. But Kefalonia is famous for its strange stories and naturally Caves couldn't be missing from here. The most significant ones are Drogorati (in Chaliomata) and the Cave of Melissani in Sami. Thanks to the lake that there is in the inside (and even more the islet within the lake (!), the Cave of Melissani is the most impressive one.

Let's see now the towns of this big island. Firstly Argostoli, the capital, set in an exceptional location but built and spread without the slightest prohibition, something that we see quite often in this country. On the other side of the same gulf, there is the rival opponent, Lixouri, less "capital" and certainly more likeable. These two towns, as happens often in Greece with nearby towns, are in a sort of informal (and once foolish) competition. I hope that, in the years that have passed since my last visit there, the intensity of this rivalry has decreased but I really doubt it. Of course, the traveller doesn't care about that. Besides, he may choose Sami (with its own port on the opposite side of the island) which may interest him more as here they have been shot the most impressive scenes of the movie that I mentioned earlier. Connection with all places mentioned above is made by ferry boat which begins, like in the case of Zakynthos, from Kyllini in Peloponnesus and also connects the two islands. The ferry passes from Poros as well, a rather large village but I shall select for the traveller some even smaller ones: Karavomilos and Agia Efthimia in the east side, Pesada in the south, Fiskardo (which most people like) in the north side, all coastal villages. Still, my nicest memory from Kefalonia is comprised of the villages located almost in a row in the area south of the center of the island, such as Valsamata, Metaxata, Rozata, Karavados and mainly Kourkoumelata. Magical memories of small, totally white and clean whitewashed houses, full of beautiful gardens. As I had the chance to realize, this was not just a childish memory (that time usually makes look better), fortunately it still is a reality. A visit to Kefalonia would even worth it to see just these!

Lefkada

Lefkada

Lefkada surely is the island that I prefer the most among the Ionian islands, but the way someone chooses an island is always a very personal and sometimes complicated affair. It's like choosing partner, isn't it? In this case also, things sometimes become complicated and other times are very simple. Love at first sight? This is not the case of Lefkada as the Aegean has better ways to seduce you straightaway. Here we are talking about an island where you go by… car. No ship, no white-dressed landscape, with still sleepy scarce lights in the first light of the dawn. Forget of the romance of the first contact with the island. Yes, but the coin has two sides: an island, not the beautiful but completely "mainland" Evvia, not the vast –for our standards- Peloponnesus but an island, a true island which connects with the ashore by a narrow lane of land. After all, it is not that bad first meeting someone without a lot of effort, is it? Just think: no ships, no stormy sea, no expensive and tasteless ship food, no squeezing in your way out… if I go on like that, I will renounce the ships which I love more than the seamen do.

What about the romance? They say that Agios Nikitas (I leave the town of Lefkada for now but I will come back) is the perfect place for those in love. That is why you should not believe everything you hear. I've been there with the wrong woman –or maybe it was the right woman in the wrong place, I don't know. But these holidays was a real (emotionally speaking) disaster. Agios Nikitas with the truly exceptional beach scarred by the Beast, does not at all permit us experience the lonely aspect that couples, at least in the beginning, need. The beach was too crowded, the stores were too crowded, the room –because of the fragile walls- had open acoustic access to many people and we were quarrelling all the time for completely irrelevant and unimportant reasons. In cases like this, the best solution is to keep on wandering. Porto Katsiki was –at that time not very easily accessible- really impressive while Syvota was so windy that any surfer would love, but we were not surfers. We arrived to the cosmopolitan Nydri –

right across the once famous Skorpios (=Scorpio), Aristotle Onassis' island, recently sold to a Russian billionaire- but also there, in Nydri, the too many people were not our cup of tea. So, returning to the town (which looks pretty much like any other provincial town in Greece) was inevitable. It is a nice town with many beautiful houses although several were deserted or abandoned. There, we regained our urban habits and completely lost the island aura. Still, it wasn't that bad. It was just different. And these were only some aspects of Lefkada. For your journey to Lefkada, I recommend a maritime excursion to Lefkata cape where there is the temple of Apollo and definitely to the quite big island Meganisi (=Mega Island) (right on the opposite side of Nydri) where the locals claim that is incomparably more beautiful than Lefkada (which they hardly like!) and they are not totally wrong: it surely worth a visit. The same stands for Papanikolis' Cave which is quite near but it requires a separate excursion, always by boat.

There are other interesting spots in Lefkada but the most important is the one that there is everywhere. The green feature. Common ground for the Ionian islands of course but still, one more reason to visit the island. I wish you to be luckier than I was. Our affair came to eanend few months later. Certainly I should not blame the island for that.

Corfu (Kerkyra, in Greek)

Corfu is the one of the three more touristic islands in Greece. A lot smaller than Crete and Rhodes, still it manages to compete with them in arrivals every summer. Corfu is not even the largest island of the Ionian islands but it is one of the most densely populated in the Mediterranean. The history of the island passes through the Homeric narrations, most of you probably remember the encounter of Odysseus and Nausica in the island of Phaeacians, right before the long-cherished return after having thought of the possibility of staying in the country of the Phaeacians, that is to say Corfu. But not all the historians agree that it really was Corfu. Most of them say that it might be the island of Scheria. Anyway, the thing is, that you don't have this kind of problems, as Odysseus, you can stay as much as you like in Corfu and return to your personal Ithaca —or have a trip to the real one, it is very close. But let's stay to Corfu. There is no doubt that thanks to its history, it is a genuinely cosmopolitan island which has received influences from the Western Europe more than any other island in Greece. These influences —this is how we call them now, before they were just conquests—hardly concern the Turkish. Corfu, like all Ionian islands, had always had strong relations with the opposite Italy but it passed to the French sovereignty, especially during the French Revolution, while at some point the Russians had also power on the island but mainly the English (the Ionian islands were united with Greece about 150 years ago, in 1864). These constant occupations and changes of sovereignty had a strong effect on its character.

You realize that as soon as you look for a while its exceptional monuments: Kanoni (=Canon) and Mon Repo, the old palace of the Brigadier Michael and Agios Georgios, Kapodistrias Hall, the metropolitan hall, the current City hall, the Ionian Academy Hall, Achilleio (Queen Elisabeth's palace) as well as the big squares —something sadly rare in Greece and not just in the islands. Spianada Square, across the Old Fort, "souvenir" from the French period, is one of the largest in the country —you can even watch cricket matches there, when in the majority of the squares in Greece you can only see parked cars. The entire Old Town of Corfu, with Liston complex standing out, is a sight. We shall also mention the church of Agios Spyridonas, one of the most significant post-byzantine monuments in the town, the Old Castle or Fortezza, an architectural masterpiece as well as the New Fort of Corfu (Fortezza Nuova) in the hill of Agios Markos which was built by the Venetians in the 16th century.

Of course, we should not forget of the beaches, plenty of fine sand (Ai Gordis, the enormous beach of Almyros, Glyfada, Sidari, Arachavi) and others that satisfy all tastes. There are more isolated ones such as Ermones or in a distance from the town, Agios Stefanos and especially in the northwest, the beach of Arillas, Ai Giorgis ton Pagon (St George of Ice) and the busy Palaiokastritsa, near the touristic homonymous village. You will find something different in Alyki of Lefkimi, Sidari with the Canal D' Amour, a hole in the rock in the sea, a tunnel, ideal for the ones in love. Tradition says that whoever swims through this passage, will find the perfect love or something like that, I don't remember well (those who are in this situation –in love- may believe anything while I have been to Corfu only in different aspects of family vacations, therefore I don't believe anything of all these). Two more options in the north: the beach of Astrakeri and Drastis' Cape (=Perpetrator's Cape) which only because of the name worth at least having a look.

A tour in the inland (it goes without saying that because of its size and the number of sights, the use of a car is obligatory) with many picturesque villages and landscapes of great natural beauty. To return to tradition, Corfu is famous for its music, from serenades to the glorious "Philharmonic" which accompanies the litany of the Epitaph in Holy Friday. A visit to Corfu during Easter is a special experience. But just for once, although normally I don't refer to the cuisine of an island –we can talk about cuisine and not just for some traditional recipes like elsewhere- with the history effect remaining vivid on the table of the people of Corfu, with "pastitsada", "sofrito", "bourdeto", "madoles" and "pastel". Among the products of local production, you will find bergamot (for sweet preserves and liquors), graviera cheese and butter of Corfu, olive oil and oregano. Don't forget to try the traditional refreshment of Corfu. It is called tsitsibyra by the English words ginger and beer. It has the flavor of ginger but not at all beer, preservatives while it constitutes the most pleasant memory from the period of the English occupation of the island. With or without it, the taste of Corfu is sweet.

south Crete

Samaria gorge, Crete

174

175

Gavdos

CRETE

So we arrived at the last stop of this journey. This island, Crete, is called megalonissos (big island) and it is indeed the biggest island, with the known exceptions of Evvia and the Peloponnese, which opted for the trail of the land. Cyprus is another story. We will stop at Crete. I will tell you few things about Crete, just because I know a lot. This is the bet. I was born here, my parents were born here, all my ancestors from what I know have been born here, my daughter was born here, and me, after many years in Athens I am back again and I live here –if I can say that I permanently live somewhere. So, what happens with an island which is almost the story of your own life?

I do not know how the story goes with others –actually I do and I detest the bad side of love of the Cretans for Crete, it is also known as chauvinism. I also know the good side of love for Crete. I tried to make it mine. See her and love her, without losing touch of what is real and mythical, without forgetting what it has to offer (a lot) and without ignoring the not so good aspects of life here. All this introduction in order to tell you, as concisely as possibly, what I would like for you to see and what to avoid in Crete. Very briefly, I will mention ten things or so that you must do in Crete so that you feel that you at least do the basics. These ten things are: the Venetian town of Chania and its port, the Samaria gorge, Elafonisi (Deer Island) and Gramvousa, the villages of the area of Sfakia, the old town of Rethymno, Mount Psiloritis and the Ideo, Knossos, Festos, Gortis in Heraklion and the plateau of Lasithi. I will add now, if you have the time and the mood (and you should find both or come to Crete another time) another ten things that will not be found easily in the guides, but I think that they are essential in order to really feel what Crete is. So I would suggest that you see at Chania, the village Milies (Apple trees) with the traditional settling that was there, especially during the winter, the villages Margarites (Daisies) and the ancient town of Eleftherna at Rethymno, the part of Southern Crete at the same municipality, from Preveli to Aghios Pavlos (if you have time do not stay in the beginning and the end of this route, others have managed to make these parts way too touristic for your taste), the village Vianos in the continuation of the Southern part towards Lasithi, that area of municipality and then, in the interior, as many villages of the plateau of Amari as you can. I would also recommend, especially if the gorge of Samaria seems a bit long, making an excursion at the gorges of Myli (Mills) at Rethymno (we can't forget of course the emblematic Monastery of Arkadion about 20 km from town), but also the gorges of Aradena (near Sfakia) and do not miss the Aghiofaraggo (Holy gorge) at the south part of Heraklion prefecture. Also the Ha gorge, at the eastern part but only if you are fit enough for it. You should not venture this latter, almost no one can cross it -unless you are an expert, so you do not need my advice. Among all of these I add, although I am not used to do so, a tip concerning food. You can choose the restaurants that bear the Cretan Cuisine Badge of Certification. They are really what they claim to be.

Now, if you leave from Heraklion, I would suggest that you take a walk in the square of Liontarion (Lions) strolling to the Venetian port. I think you have to spend some time in the Arceaological Museum, and perhaps visit Kazantzakis museum in a village not far from the town. I like Heraklion, although Chania is by far more beautiful town, and Rethymno would be an idyllic town (without the huge scars of the Beast).

Anyway, there are nice and bad things in Crete. Whoever just sees only the first, he is co-responsible for the others. That is what I think. This has nothing to do with the guide, but Crete is an island where animals are tortured in a terrible way –I am talking about puppies. In addition, in mountain areas (not in all of them, of course), there are twelve-year-old kids whose father proudly presents them with the steering wheel of the truck or tractor or the "hog" (gourouna in Greek) –if you do not what this is, it is the worst kind of motorbike ever invented with horrible volume and sound. Let's do not mention guns. Let's talk about something funnier. Last year in Chania a woman cut a tree (of the pavement) down because she wanted to park her car. All right, compared to the rest, it is funny. But it shows how widely spread the idea of *"live and let the others cut their throat –especially when they are not my relatives"* is in the island. Crete is this one as well. As well as all the nice, amazing places which are here. As well as the complete contrary mentality *"my house is always open to everyone"*, this is still there and survives even during these hard times. There are people who will be your friends after the first raki (all right, the second one) who will buy you drinks –and do not say no, especially if you are found in a mountain village. There are people who have not heard of the terms ecology, meditation, and internal harmony whereas they live in complete identification with the nature, they have the gift of real wisdom and have, without pursuing it, archived the complete balance between their desires and their soul. Apart from these, there are sceneries in Crete, I have mentioned before, where you feel you cannot help it but feel, that life in this world has some real meaning. Fortunately.

Something else, now that we are concluding: You will realize that I forgot to mention anything concerning the Northern part of Crete, apart from the big towns. True, dear traveller, I forgot to mention anything about the Northern part. Really I do not know what is wrong with me and I disregarded to introduce you the slightest bit of northern part. I cannot be forgiven. You can find though, everything can be found in the Total Guide of the Lazy Tourist. I am not the one to write it, anyway.

GAVDOS

This is a small island at the far end of the south, literally the southernmost part of Europe, a paradise for free campers. Gavdos is really the only place in Greece where free camping is not prohibited and, what's more, it is "protected" as, years ago, free campers were the only tourists of the island. Years passed, the free campers are still here, some of them staying all summer and even in the autumn, but now there are also hotels and rooms for rent. Still the character of Gavdos, the island of Caypso, remains more or less the same. A place in the sun for campers and nudists. I suggest the beaches of Sarakiniko (family friendly) Agios Ioannis (campers' paradise) Lavrakas (nudists only, please) and Tripiti – great opportunity for an excursion at the south part- where you can find a giant wooden chair, to sit and enjoy the view -a real throne and a symbol of the southernmost edge of Europe!.

A very interesting monument is also the Lighthouse (built in 1880) at the southwest side. In Gavdos we organized the first and second Sand Festivals and that was a dream come true. You will understand our choice only when you get there!(more details:https://sandfestival.wordpress.com/)

My dear traveller, I will leave you here. It was nice to travel together, I hope that now you can travel for real, on your own or with people you love. I should go, I live here and it's time to go back home. It goes without saying, till the next trip.

EPILOGUE

You step out into the deck and then you feel it for the first time. The saltiness, the sour aroma of the sea, the ship with the rust running through its veins, a floating country full of little human obsessions. Summer obsessions and fantasies. These are always the best. Everyone, including you, is trying to get used to the journey in the sea. And – pretend that know what travelling is. But every time is always like the first time. You pick a seat, you look all around you, and the journey has already started.

Then the port leaves out of your sight. Across you, with extraordinarily big and so cute, though, black sunglasses, maybe a white dog as well, she will be there reading a book. You fantasise that she pretends to be reading your book, although in the meantime she just want to find a pretext to talk to you.But the journey is what happens when we plan something else. You never get where you want to, but it does not matter. You forget about it when you see the coloursof the day slowly fading.

At night the sea is gentler and the corridors in the ship full of sleeping bags and weird dreams –in the morning the ship stewards will carefully pick up their leftovers. In the melancholic halls of the ship, people abandon themselves to the buzzing of the television and wait. Nothing is crystal clear anymore, but it is night and it is summer. It is harder to be sad about things during the summertime.

In the meanwhile, you will have seen the lights on the island –the day has not worn its clothes just yet. You know that it is more magical than the summer itself. Even more magical than the sudden rain that you might encounter tomorrow, leaning on a dry stone wall while gazing at the sea thinking about your life.

There, in the island lies a new life for you. Every time there is a fresh possibility of life here, even if you come here for years and you feel even older than the island itself. Islands never grow old anyway. Because they can simply change. So can you. That is why you travel. If something has a meaning that is travelling. Without necessarily thinking about the meaning.

Then there is the sun, the heat, the voices, drifting away in the aura of the time. There is a Greek summer, beautiful as a promise and simple as naked feet on the sand. This summer is found beyond the freshly painted signs and fake smiles. It is something that as with all the unique things cannot be put into words. You, my dear traveller, will find the way. That is what matters.

Gregory Papadoyiannis was born in Crete in 1961. He has a university degree in law and journalism, and also studied film directing.

His career history includes work with newspapers, magazines, radio and television for well-known broadcasting organisations and television stations, initially as a sports correspondent and later as a columnist and editor and has collaborated in redacting various travel guides.

At the same time he was worked as a translator, working in collaboration with prominent publishing houses. He was also active within the realm of theatre. In 1991 he received the top national award for new playwrights. He also wrote a novel, a short stories collection and a comic album.

Gregory is a co-founder, administrator and writer for the books & cinema section of the website www.eyelands.gr . He is the curator for the only Greece-based international short story competition, run by www.eyelands.gr . He also co-ordinates and leads a series of workshops on creative and collaborative writing all over Greece. After living in Athens for several years, he now lives in the island of Crete. He currently works as a translator and editor for StrangeDaysBooks Publishing (www.strangedaysbooks.gr) His novel «The baby Jazz» released in USA from Fomite books in February 2017.

52 eyelands: a genre-busting guide to the Greek Islands

Book review by LANE ASHFELDT

I never take a guidebook on my travels. That way, I don't have to worry about the long lists of things I need to 'cover' (and which, invariably, I will fail to do). But if I ever revisit the Greek Islands, I might just be packing my copy of Gregory Papadoyiannis's genre-busting guidebook 52 eyelands. Far from stressing you out with detailed lists, Papadoyiannis offers only the lightest touch of "must sees". In fact, among the book's top tips for travel is the refreshing advice to set aside all guidebooks or maps as soon as you can, and trust your instincts instead. Papadoyiannis is a Greek author, a native of the island of Crete. Although he has been visiting the Greek islands each summer for decades, he is a slow traveller, and still has a couple of dozen islands left to see.
August 30, 2013

Lane Ashfeldt *is the author of SaltWater (Liberties Press, 2014) a collection of a dozen short stories and a novella ("An impressive debut collection" The Incubator). Other stories by Lane have appeared in anthologies and magazines, among them Dancing With Mr Darcy, Guardian.co.uk, Identity Theory, Punk Fiction, Southword, The Bohemyth, and The London Magazine. Visit Lane online at: ashfeldt.com*

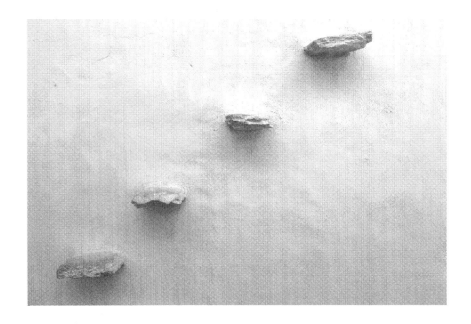

185

Amorgos

STRANGE DAYS BOOKS

Strange Days Books is a cooperative publishing organization based in Crete, Greece.

We publish books by young writers from Greece but we also publish books by writers from around the world. In the past seven years of our existence we have published Greek translations of books by writers from countries such as the USA, England, Spain, Bulgaria. For many of these authors this was their first book ever to be published! Strange Days Books also publish first releases of books by foreign authors in English!

For the past seven consecutive years, Strange Days Books & eyelands.gr coordinate the only international short story contest based in Greece. We publish low cost digital editions and our books are distributed mainly through the internet but also through bookstores and cooperative bookshops. Some of our publications are also available in kindle format from amazon.com and in e-book format from smashwords.com

Strange Days Books is an entirely independent publisher, primarily interested in showcasing the wealth of the new writing voices of Greece. We work closely with our authors in order to create books that will appeal to booklovers, books about the present, books contemporary readers can relate to, books that strive to push the art of literature forward, books written with talent and passion, books that challenge the way we see the world, books that burst with new ideas and intriguing perspectives, books that have something to say and were not written for merely commercial purposes. In other words, we create books with character together, steadily growing into a community of artists and art-lovers that represent and promote the truly new literature of Greece, not only through publishing but also through a literary festival, the only international short story competition in Greece, theatrical play and novel competitions, book events and more.

Every summer we organize Sand Festival - a literary festival held literally on the sand of one of the Greek Islands.

Eyelands.gr literary magazine in collaboration with Strange Days Books organize an annual international short story competition, which is the only international short story contest based in Greece. Every year, writers from all the continents of the world participate in it. The competition consists of two categories; Greek and International (for the international section we only accept stories in English). Running continuously since 2010, offers hundreds of writers the opportunity to see their short story printed in one of our collections, created through the contest entries. For many of these writers it is the first time that a story of theirs is printed in a book or featured online. The jury reads all submissions blind. The English section of the competition has been recognized as a truly reliable, fair and serious short story competition.

EYELANDS BOOK AWARDS
In 2018 Strange Days Books & Eyelands.gr decided it was time to launch Eyelands Book Awards and Three Rock Writers' Residency Program. The former is an international contest that gives the opportunity to a writer to win a great prize; a holiday in Athens, Greece, where he/she will have the chance to talk about his/her work to Greek readers and meet Greek writers in a special ceremony and also gives the opportunity to an unpublished writer to win a contract and see her/his book published by Strange Days Books. It was high time for Greece to have an international book award.

THREE ROCK WRITERS' RESORT RESIDENCY PROGRAM
Three Rock Writers' Resort Residency is a self-directed program that offers time and space for writers to work on a creative project of their choice and above all an extraordinary opportunity to enjoy life on Crete.
Writers in all creative writing genres are invited to apply. Novels, plays, short stories, poetry, graphic novel, everything is eligible. Our residency is designed for emerging and established writers seeking to dedicate a period of time to a project in any genre.
You may choose to stay in a single or shared apartment or in your private studio, at an already well known resort for award-winning writers from everywhere in the world, who have been our guests since 2012. Space is also available for one partner/friend writers would like to bring along at no extra cost

*Milos,
Klima*

STRANGE DAYS BOOKS
Editions in English

Σειρά: Αγγλόφωνες εκδόσεις

52 eyelands, a sentimental guide through the Greek islands
Kindle version, 2013
by Gregory Papadoyiannis
Slowly but thoroughly
by Ben D. Fischer
The Time collection
Eyelands 4th International Short Story Contest
The short listed stories
Borderline stories
Eyelands 5th International Short Story Contest
The short listed stories
Stories in colour
Eyelands 6th International Short Story Contest
The short listed stories
Strange Love Affairs
Eyelands 7th International Short Story Contest
The short listed stories
Luggage
Eyelands 8th International Short Story Contest
The short listed stories
Dreams
Eyelands 1st International Flash Fiction Contest
44 dreamy stories from all over the world

Strange Days Books
Social Cooperative Publishing House
Address: Chimarras 6, Rethymno, 74100, tel: +2831503835
email: strangedaysbooks@gmail.com
twitter https://twitter.com/paraxenes_meres
www.paraxenesmeres.gr
www.strangedaysbooks.gr
www.facebook.com/STRANGEDAYSBOOKS
Sand Festival: https://sandfestival.wordpress.com/
Creative Writing Workshop: https://strangedaysworkshops.wordpress.com/

Printed in Great Britain
by Amazon

35918782R00118